Harold Whit Williams

SELECTED POEMS

FUTURECYCLE PRESS

www.futurecycle.org

Cover photo, Harold Whit Williams' electric guitar, by Ashley Savage Williams; cover and interior design by Diane Kistner; Gentium Book Basic text and Cronos Pro titling

NOTE

Except for stylistic differences, the poems appear as published in the represented collections.

Library of Congress Control Number: 2023945401

Published by FutureCycle Press
Athens, Georgia, USA

ISBN 978-1-952593-43-7

Contents

from
RED CLAY JOURNAL

from
MY HEAVENS

from
A RAIN ANCESTRAL

NEW POEMS

Foreword

I don't write poetry anymore. When I did, though—for the same reason I still read it—it was to connect with others who knew their present moment was already gone and had left paper trails. Verbal handprints on the cave walls of vanished here-and-nows.

As Walt Whitman put it two long lifespans ago:

> Just as you feel when you look on the river and sky, so I felt,
> Just as any of you is one of a living crowd, I was one of a crowd.

Or the son of the assistant director of the Japanese Bureau of Horses, Minamoto no Shitago, a thousand years earlier:

> This world—
> To what may I liken it?
> To autumn fields
> lit dimly in the dusk
>
> by lightning flashes

Or the late, great astronomer Carl Sagan the year before I was born:

> Writing is perhaps the greatest of human inventions, binding together people, citizens of distant epochs, who never knew one another. Books break the shackles of time.

Or the space villain in Alex Garland's sci-fi screenplay, *Sunshine:*

> At the end of time, a moment will come when just one man remains. Then the moment will pass. Man will be gone. There will be nothing to show that we were ever here...but stardust.

Which brings us to Harold Whit Williams, whose poetry paints with each of these colors, often simultaneously, always masterfully. For Whit, impermanence is colored with sadness:

> I am
> Staring down the hall
> Into Mother's room. Her journals,
>
> Her jewelry, her hair on the pillow
> A light that we see
> We think we see. It soon enough fades,
> And we forget.

And longing:

In this voice you hear
Church hymnal pages turn,

A merry-go-round squeak,
Summer downpours on a tin roof.

And history:

On this day bus to Dublin. So many names.
So many names stacked
Like gray stones in the fallow fields.
And those green hills rising up,
Daring us to believe in them.

But also the everyday:

The morning is, whether I want it to be or not.

The grocery list an epic poem.

And gallows humor:

You are all winners!
I shout to those cold wet headstones.
No one is watching,

So I foxtrot past the graveyard,
Whistling. I just did it.

And a hybrid sad absurdity:

The dream is real. My father is real.
He scans the hometown daily
For dead people he might know.
He keeps outdated food in the fridge
To stay connected to the past.
The past is never past,
It's not even ketchup anymore.

Wave back
At Lloyd, son, he baited your hooks.
He let you ring up the cash register.
His wife Martha wiped your ass once.

In short, like those who came before him, Whit, while he's still here, while we are—is "trying to describe / A childhood summer pasture, and how at dusk / Lightning bugs suddenly appear above sagegrass." He, too, is "gearing up / For all that future nothingness." And for anyone who has ever felt the way the other, deader Whit (Whitman) felt looking at rivers and skies, these poems are a fine addition to your personal library of books that will someday decompose into soil like our bodies.

If gallows humor isn't your cup of tea, though, fear not! There's also the gallows without humor (see: "future nothingness" above + "all the days of the years / Curve out before each of us, / A deep-rutted gravel road going nowhere"), as well as humor without the gallows (see: the singer with the haircut from Oasis burping and grabbing his nuts).

If this feels scattershot, I'm with you. To again quote a writer better than myself (again Whit):

> Guess I'm not making myself clear. If only
> I had perfect pitch and a dead composer's
> Powdered wig. If only I could sing exactly
> What I want to say.

What I want to say, I think, is that Whit's poetry, like his music, resonates on many (often AM/FM radio) frequencies. There's music in rain on leaves. And cicadas in distorted guitars. There's rock 'n' roll and shrieking preachers and ghosts in tape hiss. Small pox and Southern gothic and philosophical beard talk. Birdsong and songbirds. Woodsmoke and weed smoke. Lightning bugs and porch lights. Gods and goddamnits and tater tots.

At heart, though, vivid and musical as they are, these are poems of memory and acceptance. The *suburban* in his poem "Suburban Ephemera" (*My Heavens*) seems less the setting of the poetry and more the setting of the poet. A midlife suburbanite at home, unsticking himself from time. Looking back to a more rural Alabaman adolescence: a here-and-now vanished into a there-and-then. And glimpsing a future of eerily (enviably) untroubling nothingness. All the while rooted in the beauty, the tragedy, the comedy, the monotony, the everything of the moment.

Scott Alexander Jones
Vinohrady, Prague
Friday, September 30, 2022, 9:27 a.m.
49°F. *Broken clouds. More clouds than sun.*[1]

[1]www.timeanddate.com/weather/czech-republic/prague

from
WAITING FOR THE FIRE TO GO OUT

Finishing Line Press, 2011

Wisdom in a Pond Reflection

For Wang Wei, Claude Monet, and Billy Gibbons

My beard outgrows me.

Born Homecoming Friday

There are certain things one misses
From back east, from down south—

Catbirds calling in kudzu tangle
Or perfume of magnolia

On the bare neck of a summer evening.
Confederate fife and drum songs

Rattling up from red clay
As a gray fox haunts the backyard.

Thick fog of cigar smoke
And a flash of cheerleader panties

At the high school football game.
A mother's voice becoming a spoon

Clinking in her mother's cast iron skillet.
A newborn's cry, a plum-sized raindrop.

Clipped lawns sleeping in sunlight
And the way afternoons pass

In the pace of a grandmother's drawl.
How a creek named Little Bear

Floats my words downstream
Before I can even think to write them.

The dead burying us daily.

Early Recordings Vol. 1

The first thing you notice
Is tape hiss,

A wavy analog breath
Building into cicada buzz.

Your Christian name
Displayed in spidery cursive

On a yellowed cassette cover.
A man mumbles, blue jays shriek.

A child's voice chimes in—
Deep South inflections,

Honeysuckle sweet
And pine sap dripping.

In this voice you hear
Church hymnal pages turn,

A merry-go-round squeak,
Summer downpours on a tin roof.

It responds to the man mumbles
With bird sounds and giggles.

You press rewind, play repeatedly,
Hearing the swish of corduroy.

False Spring

O orchid tree, your pale blossoms
Perfume my daydreams.
Your beard of bees
Hums my high school fight song.

O distant skyscraper, your metal face
Shines like Y2K New Year's Eve.
Your tower warning signal
Pulses my wedding day EKG.

O sacred bus stop, your rusted bench
Weeps and gnashes its teeth.
Your darkened streetlight
Totems my stillborn brother's face.

O palm tree, I love you most of all!
Your regal fronds pity us all—

The wandering, the rootless.

Confessions of a Southern Dandy

If you happen to find me lingering
On your front porch with the phone ringing,
Teakettle whistling, so on and so forth,

Just know that I'm trying to describe
A childhood summer pasture, and how at dusk
Lightning bugs suddenly appear above sage grass,

Hovering like tiny U.F.O.s in the honeysuckle air.

And please forgive my mushmouth dialect,
I'm simply mimicking a bobwhite, or a coonhound,
Or granddaddy gumming hot buttered corn on the cob.

And pay no mind to that shaky hand up your skirt,
That's either a re-enactment of Bull Run,
Or last night's winning Crimson Tide touchdown,

Depending on how much bourbon was poured.

And for Christ sakes, don't be offended
By my lack of eye contact,
Seems these days I'm always looking up,

Trying to see the sky beyond the sky.

The Glass Ceiling

In a summer field
Of blooming Mexican hats
And oxblood lilies
I glimpse your ghost

Crouching
Then pouncing

Scattering sparrows
Like windgusted leaves
And casting no shadow
Under noonday sun

But you only dreamed
Of scattered sparrows
From that warm windowsill

And those
Are not sparrows anyway
But invoice slips

And you are not in
A summer field
But an autumn cubicle
Breathing in minutes

And exhaling days

Reply to Li Po on My 41st Birthday

My ears sprout old man fuzz.
I listen to rain music on oak leaves

But lyrics still elude me.

Ribs long to be licked clean
And bleached by summer sun.

Knees creak like grandfather stairs.

Shoulders sag under the massive bulk
Of one more gray afternoon.

In my belly, a thousand bottles of wine.

Cold, selfish hands, shaking,
Grab for more and more of nothing.

Where does my hair go at night?

Blood Brothers

We were Cherokee and Chickasaw
In Old Mose's pasture,
Warring in the sage grass
That danced in south wind.
Standing by the blackberry bramble
As if in church, Tom
Sliced his palm with a pocketknife.
He held aloft the bloody hand,
Gave me the knife and I did the same.
With our wounds pressed tight,
A crow cawed thrice
From the woods atop Gacky Hill,
And we both admitted in whispers
That it stung just a little.

Indian Summer Detour

Sway of sunlit goldenrod.
Was it this house, or the next?

All that remains is the wood frame,
Butter churn filled with fire ants

And someone's disembodied ancestor.
A Confederate ghost

Raking newly fallen dogwood leaves.
Not a soldier per se, more likely

A medic, a hand-holder,
Giver of morphine to the dying and insane.

Leaf piles scatter in south wind.
Across Old Memphis highway

Bluegill pop on a pond surface
And the setting sun whispers my secrets

To the other side of the world.

Waiting for the Fire to Go Out

Each day we give our words to wind.
        Watch them disperse among the woodsmoke.

Words like *yes, no, maybe, ornithology,*
        And the Spanish word for owl, which is *búho.*

The owl I saw as a child is long dead
        But that doesn't stop me scanning treetops at dusk.

Tonight, our dying star sun lingers in the live oak
        And grandfather's rifle is a day's drive from here.

from
BACKMASKING

Texas Review Press, 2014
Robert Phillips Poetry Chapbook Winner

Call to Prayer

O heavenly make-believe father, hear thy doves
Cooing on this ninety-degree winter day. See thy
Early buds flash pink and purple for all those bees
You did not create. Forgive me, thy doubting son,
For this afternoon, as I almost spied your shadow
Shadowing mine down a sunstricken sidestreet
Behind that church I always pass, but someday
Might enter. We all tell ourselves the craziest things.
Like—forgive and forget, do unto others, love
The one you're with, in-a-gadda-da-vida. And
Just between the two of us, I'm not so sure
You're even up there at all, nosy-neighboring,
Peeking out behind silver cloud-curtains,
Taking down tag numbers and calling the cops.
But in case you are, thanks for the aroma of coffee,
The slow striptease of sunset, for thunderstorms—
So reassuring from a distance. Thanks for the way
Women cross and uncross their legs, the way
Live oak branches dip and sway in balmy breezes,
Their greenfingers turning tiny pages of twilight,
The way we dream you, then forget upon awakening.

Tracking the New Record

Hays County, Texas 2012

Old J can fall asleep at will. He nods
And droops as R begins to fuss with loony
Machines and patching cords. We bow our heads
When D intones a prayer to Bonham, Moonie,
The like. I'm feeling peckish, dizzy, feeble.
A cactus wren beyond the window flits
And calls. I stomp my octave fuzz to tweedle
Replies. A thunderclap, then intro beats
To count the jangle in. As R recalls
A joke into the microphone, he tunes,
Then turns to hit record. The chiming bells
Of Telecasters; blustery bass and drums.
My godamighty! That'll cause a stir—
Says R. I yawn and long to cut my hair.

Liam Gallagher, Uninterpreted, Backstage

Bataclan, Paris, France 2000

Beside this millionaire, I stammer, cough
And tell him I'm a fan. We spy a crowd
Below who've Channel-hopped; these thugs with rough
And tumble voices croaking English-proud
Huzzahs and soccer chants. Someone is waving
The Union Jack as Liam laughs and mutters
Mancunian questions, alleyway threats. Swigging
His pint, he waits for me to speak. I offer
A shrug and mumble something Darwin wrote
About the origin of species. Liam
Adjusts his nuts and belches—fookin' great!
The chanting volume swells. I think of home,
Cicada droning summer heat. His grunts
Give words I catch, like—Learjet, London, cunt.

Fame Studio Session

Muscle Shoals, Alabama 1989

Its history in rock and roll was lost on me
The night that we snuck in. My buddy Jon
Had called a friend who'd let us tape for free.
The evening band had paid, was packed and gone
When we arrived with drums, guitars and Tom—
His blank cassettes would dub our only tune.
I can't recall who played the bass, or hum
The hooks and riffs we tracked. So, pretty soon
We called it quits, our demo done. I'd love
To say we felt Aretha's vibe, or heard
That Wilson Pickett preacher-scream above
Our own pathetic din. But clever words
And chords are not enough. Beside our cars
We lingered in the lot and spoke of stars.

Villanelle for Bloodbait

The stench rises to our sunburnt noses
As daddy shouts out—my lord, that's loud—
And once opened, the jar never closes.

We slop it on hooks as granddaddy dozes
Then wakes to say—them catfish ain't proud.
The stench rises to our sunburnt noses

To blot out odor from those knockout roses
Blooming near the pond in a thorny crowd.
And once opened, the jar never closes—

A Pandora's box of stink; what decomposes
To make this mess we all wonder aloud.
The stench rises to our sunburnt noses

To hang in the air as my cane-pole imposes
Its weight on my thin boy-arms unendowed.
And once opened, the jar never closes.

A gullywasher'd be nice—daddy supposes
To a white sky with no prayer of a cloud.
The stench rises to our sunburnt noses
And once opened, the jar never closes.

My First Rally

I'd like to say it was for peace
Or raising workers' wages,
Or that the next-door neighbors' boy
Coerced me into going
Instead of staying home to play
With army men and Legos.
But there I walked, quite willingly,
Beside him among the pines.
I'd like to think that all those faces
Made a multiethnic rainbow,
And not the storm of sunburnt scowls
Twisted in a sweaty rage.
We pushed up front to see, then waved
For panning TV cameras.
A red-robed man dripped through the mass
Of white sheets and hoods
Like a drop of blood from an open wound.
He stooped to take a torch
Then set fire to a plywood cross.
The crowd cheered, and I recalled
A National Geographic saying
Jesus was African, ebony-skinned,
Wiry-haired. I pictured Him
Up there, roasting and shrieking.
The red-robed man spoke. His voice,
Raspy, punctuated by applause,
Boomed from the stage's loudspeakers
Like an old world truth. We left
Before the crowd broke up, before
The cross flamed out. And later,
At home, daddy paddled me hard.
Each whack upon my backside
He said, was for all I'd seen and heard.
He even gave a few extra licks
For things burned in his memory
That he'd long tried to forget.

Playing Along with "Are You Experienced," Backwards Guitar Solo

Colbert County, Alabama 1987

Just months before he passes, buddy Robbie
Presents to me some Hendrix albums—Band
Of Gypsys, others. Bless his sweet and tiny
Deformed heart—my momma says. The end
Guitar—*If 6 Was 9,* from *Axis: Bold*
As Love, reverberates inside my room,
My ear canals. And then his debut record
Distorts my Chinese speakers. Outside our home
It's either day or night; it's hot or cold.
This sound is prehistoric, avian. Birds
Of old that died in pits of tar cried
Like this. I fret and follow, moan the words
And noodle out of tune. Then daddy knocks
For dinnertime. Someday I'll get these licks.

Backmasking Presentation, United Methodist Church Youth Group

Tuscumbia, Alabama 1985

The basement reeks of tater tots. Our guts
Are gurgling after Sunday dinner. Preacher
Recalls the rock and roll and sinful glut
Of youth—the Jethro Tull and Alice Cooper
And Molly Hatchet shows; the grass and wine.
He lays an album on the stereo's table
And speaks of overdoses, doing lines
Of coke and dust and smack. He drops the needle
But spins the album in reverse. The sounds
I dig are cymbals, fuzz guitar and bells
That swell and moan like magick underground.
This singer—preacher yells—is seeking hell
And wants to place your soul in Satan's hands!
I knew that night I'd have to join a band.

First Electric Guitar, Sears & Roebuck Special

Florence, Alabama 1983

My sister's steady rocks his Boston vinyl
To air-guitar the power chords. His flat
Is cramped with crates of records, amps. Aw, you'll
Be sure to dig this one—he says—my Strat
I sold the other day. The action's high;
The color's green like momma's kitchen counter.
I pick it up as sister rolls her eyes
And checks her watch. We need to leave at quarter
Of ten to get you home—she snaps. He plugs
It in a Peavey set to fuzz. It growls
And barks like Jack, our neighbor's mongrel. Gigs
Won't come along for years, much less the halls
And clubs. Applause erupts outside the door—
I'm nailing Twenty-Five Or Six To Four.

Tent Revival on Hawk Pride Mountain

Colbert County, Alabama 1980

I sit with friends from school. We dig our toes
Into the sawdust floor and pop our gum.
A band onstage commences with the show
And thumps pathetic gospel rock. A hymn
Would be appropriate, I think, but folks
Around us hoot and stomp and sing. The preacher
Appears from back behind the drums. He kicks
Like Vegas Elvis. He's fat with oily hair
And sparkled suit. My friends rise up to clap
But I stay put. The stench of stale cologne,
Perfume and sweat has made me queasy. I slap
Both hands down on my knees and gaze upon
The giant bluejeaned ass in front of me.
Where's this Holy Spirit I cannot see?

Pantoum from Wilson Pickett Interview

Mother was the baddest woman in my book.
I get scared of her now and I was raised on gospel.
She'd hit me with anything—skillets and stove wood.
One time I ran away and cried for a whole week.

I get scared of her now and I was raised on gospel
That the preacher screamed out on a Sunday morning
And one time I ran away and cried for a whole week,
Stayed in the backwoods, me and my little dog.

That preacher screamed out on a Sunday morning
Like mother kneeling down, hollering for my soul.
And I stayed in the backwoods, me and my little dog,
But God don't put no more on you than you can bear.

After mother knelt down and hollered for my soul
She'd hit me with anything—skillets and stove wood—
But God don't put no more on you than you can bear.
That mother was the baddest woman in my book.

Purchasing a First Album, Charlie Daniels Band, Saddle Tramp, Pegasus Records

Muscle Shoals, Alabama 1979

I mow the grass in neighbors' yards. The dollars
Are stuffed in a jar and hid beneath my bed.
It seems I have enough as momma hollers—
C'mon let's go to town! I catch a ride
With her, my pockets packed with green. I've had
My eyes upon a disc, its cover art
Depicts this gaudy western painting bad
Enough to grace some hippie's van. I'm smart
About my dough, I know, but this will change
My life. The freak behind the counter rings
Me up and snickers. He says—that color orange
In the sky above the gaucho looks like Tang,
The drink of astronauts. I tell him thanks,
Then take it home to find the music stinks.

Billy Sherrill Borrows Granddaddy's Martin Acoustic

Bear Creek, Alabama 1960

This fella dresses cool. His pompadour
Is longish, greasy. Menthol cigarette
And pointy shoes. So Max—he slurs—this here
Guitar will do just fine. I'm off to hit
Ol' Muscle Shoals or Nashville. Daddy shuffles
The gravel road and says—that Ottis, he
Retired from gospel singing. Into sales
Or something. Picking ain't his life. So Billy,
With sweaty brow, with baby beard, takes
The axe from Max and burns a riff. This rube
Can really play, my daddy thinks. His licks
Report like rifle fire. Been reading tab
And charts to learn the chords—he says, then sighs—
This neck is smooth as Sally's inner thighs.

Crazed Man Changes Weather

For David Wojahn

Elvis Aaron Presley, born Tupelo, Mississippi
January 8th, 1935, once used yogi mind-power
To move a single small cirrus cloud backwards
Above the death-bleak Nevada desert and for this
Was placed in the Rock & Roll Hall of Fame
Just weeks before his untimely explosion
Atop a Memphis, Tennessee toilet. And I figure
If this poor boy's deep-fried gray matter
Could command such meteorological magic,
Then what of my own humdrum, caffeine
In the morning, scotch whisky in the evening
Early to bed, Leave it to Beaver brain?
So, on an unusually warm midwinter day
With a fast approaching cold front to the north,
I stand, arms stretched out and up, in my street,
Straining like the old Hound Dog himself,
Quietly humming Return to Sender, Teddy Bear,
Love Me Tender and Suspicious Minds,
When lo and behold, the blue sky freezes
Into a full-color photocopy of itself. And as
Thousands of red-winged blackbirds rain down
I can only wish our God, our King, was still alive
To looketh upon me, verily, and tremble.

Are You Washed in the Blood?

Boar Tush, Alabama 1955

So Henry Tidwell, mother's daddy, is struck
By a neighbor's white lightning. He falls,
A-trembled, to his knees. They sink and suck
Into the reddish mud. He frowns and pulls
Another sup. Beneath his humming hive
Of bees he cries—O Lord, am I a sinner?
Too many pretty legs for me to give
Attention to! And nary a word at dinner,
Kind or otherwise, from my own woman.
Too tight, is Henry, to feel the stinging bee
Upon his neck. Another sign, an omen
Of sorts—the fallen leaves from maple trees
That pool and pond like drops from a wound.
O God! He yelps. Is your answer only wind?

Old Union Baptist Church

Winston County, Alabama 1939

A Sunday morning dawns among the pines.
The boy, my daddy, climbs into a buggy
With Uncle Clefe who smells of smoke and wine
From muscadines. He tugs the reins, that ginny
She snorts and clops along a muddy road
Towards the meeting house out by the slough.
Before too long, a mason jar he stowed
Behind the bench, it tumps on daddy's shoes
So Clefe, he barks a curse, says—bare your feet
You hear? Your mother'll tan my sorry hide
And God don't fret about us dressing neat.
Nearby the church they halt. I'll stay outside
He says as daddy mounts the splintered stairs.
Old Clefe and mule stay put to snore their prayers.

Do This in Remembrance of Me

Awake at dawn on a pine-darkened road to school.
Your skyblue child-eyes seek out Caravaggio's
Caucasian Christ in each fogbank and foreclosed
Farmhouse, each cloud-devouring cotton field.
At recess, meekness in a dodgeball game
Inherits rude rhymes for your middle name.
Turn the other cheek to see, not angelwings
In elm branches, but plastic bags caught
Snapping beatitudes in hot southwesterlies.
Sunday morning, preacher drones eternal hellfire,
The Good Book split asunder in your skinny lap.
Its tiny-fonted letters blur into bird tracks—
Northern cardinal, eastern meadowlark, those
Quail prints you followed after a rare snowfall
To the center of a frozen pond. First, they darted
Left, then right, then disappeared altogether.

A Medium-Sized Theology

For Wendell Berry

Be still and know that you are god,
Or at the very least—a stray hair,
A fragment, a cell, an atom
In some bearded deity's third eye.
Be still and know that I have a friend
Who talks only to her god
But should try talking to herself.
I talk to her—she's a friend of god
And having this connection can't hurt.
Be god and know that you are still
As a tire swing on Christmas morning.
How about this—be still and know
There is no god but this moment
And we are in this moment
Like that fallen poplar leaf,
Yellow in the sidewalk puddle
Gone gray from a lowering sky
That might or might not rain.

Mapmaking: The Early Years

So look: I've drawn this field. It marks the spot
Where morning sun will wake the larks and cattle.
One time it burned, but let's not talk of that.
Here's Thomas, shirtless, biking into battle
With arrows, bow. We track the trolls that lurk
In woods up here along this northern border
And also Chickasaw, as we are Creek.
The mileage scale and legend aren't in order
But there's the road to school. Go south, those hills
Where giant eagles hunt and roost begin
To rise. I've rendered them to size. This feels
As though it needs a stippled bog or fen.
Except for chocolate smudge, my west is blank
And bare. Someday I'll fill it in, I think.

from
LOST IN THE TELLING

FutureCycle Press, 2015

A Rum-Drunk Toast After Raking Oranges from a Neighbor's Tree, and Ending with a Banal Line from a Seventies Pop Song

To Ron Zacapa and Che Guevara, to Carmen
Miranda and our Miranda rights, to Rites
Of Spring and the Arab Spring and what we
Sing in the shower, to the meaning of your

Name and all that mine rhymes with, to
The gods of Popol Vuh, to old Chano next
Door and Banana Man on the corner, to
Your flashing Mayan temper and my inbred

British chin, to the ache in our shoulders
And the splinters we'll dig out tomorrow,
To the soft laughter of backporch women,
To the cotton candy sunset and the *beer beer*

Call of nighthawks, to the thudding of each rain-
Plumped fruit into the freshly cut St. Augustine.
O friend, *mi diablo*! Our glasses are emptied—
Nothing lasts forever but the earth and sky.

Light at the End of the Tunnel

We're nearing the part of the high school play
Where the leading man finds a letter—his lover
Long gone, bound for shimmering city lights.
We're fast approaching the final track of Side 2—

A brooding, introspective fingerpicked folk
Melody flowing into furious amp feedback.
We've dropped below a quarter of a tank, love,
And this pineywoods highway has nothing

But churches. We've awakened on our porch
And the lawn is lush from last night's rain.
In the blooming redbud tree, a sparrow sings—
I can see for miles and miles and miles and miles...

A True North Dream with Astronomy and Botanical Consequences

Somewhere along the trail, this
Flashlight becomes a femur, and I
Take that for a sign. Like when moss
Grows on the north side of trees
Except when it grows on all sides.
Or when the Big Dipper cannot
Be spotted through those freakish
Superstorm clouds. Should I mention
Sleepwalking runs in my family?
All I can say is that each day
Is a cool copse of virgin spruce
Where I forage and grow musky.
And before long, my fingers leaf out.
I become rooted beside a brook
That refuses to babble my name.
Eventually, it speaks when I bare
My spindly branches for winter.
It murmurs—All I've ever wanted
Was to find my way back home.

Gunwaleford Road Pastoral

It can all turn south in the blink of an eye,
In a flutter of bird wings, in the butterfly
Oak leaf wind gust. Once, I pulled a red wagon
That rattled with fossils; now I groan and wheeze
When the alarm sounds. Each day is either

A cloud wisp skirting the cathedral spire
Or another sandstone stacked on the burial cairn.
In geologic time, both blip past unnoticed.
They say rainfall patterns fluctuate according to

Yahweh's whimsy. This gives us plenty to discuss
At the general store. Around a woodstove
We gather with RC Colas and moon pies,
All asking the same question while using
Different tones and accents and words.

Blues Dreams

For Hubert Sumlin

Born Under a Bad Sign

Along the way somebody hefted an axe
And took some whacks against my family tree.
Those dead-branch second cousins, those
Low-hanging aunts and uncles gone
Soggy and rotten—they all had it coming.
To this day I bay like the neighbor's cur
Drunken from the fermented windfalls.
I droop and dream of Daddy's orchard,
All the shiny and soft pears and plums.
Honeybees up in the sun-bright blossoms.
Each trunk weatherworn, bug-scarred.
Each fruit wearing a face I'll fondly forget.

Mannish Boy

And another time Daddy says look
Out the window, not my window,
Your window, the one that's cracked,
The one that's half-open and hazy
From mud splatter and field grit.
The one letting in those raindrops,
Fat and salty, falling from gulf clouds.
See that crooked old house yonder
Leaning behind the Texaco pump?
They say the ghost of Lovely Lloyd
Haints the front-porch rocking chair,
Hollering and waving at fast-passing
Traffic bound for Tupelo or Jasper
Or Bear Creek or Nauvoo. Wave back
At Lloyd, son, he baited your hooks.
He let you ring up the cash register.
His wife Martha wiped your ass once.

Another Mule Kicking In My Stall

At this juncture the river is too wide,
Too swift and too strong. A bottleneck
Slide scraped along taut catgut strings
That sing and moan like a crop-beaten
Beast of burden. Cry *gee,* then cry *haw.*
Cry over evil deeds done at midnight.

What a sight! This Old Muddy flooding
Fields, lapping the levee. I'll get there
Somehow, someway, and on that day
You'll be sorry you've done me wrong.
My High John the Conqueror root,
My gris-gris bag, my thirty-eight special
Hot in my hand. I just quit that band,
Burnt down your house of blues. You
Say two of us forever, but my aim is true.

See That My Grave Is Kept Clean

Salt these wounds, my sweaty friend,
And let the noise begin with Elmore,
Blind Lemon, Muddy and all the Kings.
Men do feel the need to be useful
Even when low on gas, passed out,
Flaccid, drunk upon scuffed hardwoods.
I'll be good by tomorrow morn.
Your sneer, your scorn is my rye
Whiskey and draft beer. Do you hear
Sonny Boy's harp out of tune and yet
Perfect? Do you taste champagne, smell
The reefer? Can't you see? Sooner or
later we all live our blues. We enter
That cutting contest bound to lose.

Last Blue Yodel

Let us both huddle around
That little golden fire
Inside the whiskey bottle.

Each sip, a breath of smoke.
Let us bow, pray to weather—
That hard norther howling,

Pawing at our windows.
Let us yawn and stretch
And down the last dram.

Let the remainder of my life
Be a library paperback, one
You toss in the backseat

And never return. Let us
Nod off and snore as my
Beard goes a winter-sky gray.

Let Jimmie Rodgers skip
On our thrift store turntable—
Woman made a fool out of me...
Woman made a fool out of me...
Woman made a fool out of me...

In a Sentimental Mood

Alive as ice melts in the backyard,
Neighborhood children caterwaul
A snow day. Ever a thinking man,

Considering all sides, comers, takers—
Could just as easily be dead with ice
Popping inside a whiskey tumbler.

Bluish hands licked by the house cat.
Two crows fussing a hawk up
And out of the oak. A low hum

From speakers finished blasting
Coltrane with Ellington. No one
Around to flip over Side One.

Still Life with Gibson SG and Unpacked Bags

My fellow traveler, we should be committed!
Those days without sleep, the studio slog,
That Sisyphean loading out of abused
Equipment; luggage stolen; in the bag
To board a mid-morning London flight.
But what brave heroics, you and I—a Soho
Debut, our Radio One almost-hit,
A Marshall stack up loud to steal the show.
My blood and sweat are soaked into the wood
Around your pickup heart, your wiry veins.
A coat of paint that once was white is yellowed
From cigarette and reefer smoke and stains
Of god knows what. Let's toast the gypsy life,
The near and far misses, the trouble and strife.

A Correspondence of Sorts

After midnight, a Ouija board and I
Write you a love letter. No invisible
Ink, though, so I make quick jotting
Gestures above the brittle parchment.

No empty bottle, no ocean to drop it in, so
I stay put, as this weather's turned atrocious.
The world outside my window? It could be
Endless in the dark. I should pretend
I'm you reading this letter out loud,

But I've no matches for the candle
And no candle for the candlelight,
And whatever it was I meant to say
Can be better said by not saying it.

Lost in the Telling

When our flat-screen TV
Becomes a slash pine campfire
I will whittle you a raven
That fits in your palm.

I will spin you tight yarns
About a time before sunset
Before this world became
A dark alley with broken glass.

Some things will get lost
In the telling, other things
Will be found out too late.
The woodsmoke will sing

And your little bird will fly
And night will burn off
Like some summer fog
The dry creek dreamt up.

Winston County Bottom Feeders

The overstocked catfish pond sleeps
By Highway 43, south of Boar Tush.
In late morning heat, Daddy's daddy
Sits frail in his lawn chair. His leathery
Hands quiver a cane pole; his cracked
Talon-fingers reek of stink bait.
He whispers curses and incantations,
Beckoning the sly, whiskered creatures.
Whistling, jittery, Daddy spies swallows
Overhead, gorging on mosquitoes
Full of our just-sucked blood. Our
Go-juice, he calls it. From us to bug
To swallow to hawk to vulture to clay
To hay to Holstein, then back to us,
And where does all this end? Daddy's daddy
Drops his head to snore. Daddy hollers—
This is the day that the Lord hath made!
I scratch an elbow, itch and think—surely
This goodness and mercy shall fail me
All the days of my life, as I will dwell
In murky depths till the lure floats down,
The hook sinks in, the line draws taut...

Our Lord and Savior's Mixtape

Highway 72 slithers and slinks
Like some serpent in the garden.
A Mercury Zephyr with half a tank.
Factory tape deck blasting R.E.M,
AC/DC and The Cult. Guns &
Roses. Little traffic from here
To Tishomingo. Surprise snow
Left around the catfish ponds.
Doublewides with Xmas lights.
A church, a Texaco, another church,
A shooting range. County line
Liquor stores, another church.
Fugazi and The Meat Puppets.
What exactly would Jesus do?
Don camouflage and carry an AK?
Backhand his Mary Magdalene
After a long and pointless day
At the chicken plant? Would he
Be offended by this Zeppelin
Track or just muss up his hair
In the rearview, laughing off
The irony? Would he lust after
That slutty red-haired cheerleader?
Would he say to her, *It's no secret*
Who I am, just ask around? Would
He kill the headlights on that flat
Stretch east of Iuka? Count to ten
Before switching them back on?
Might he say, *Brother, take this,*
Thy wheel or *Do unto others*
Before they damn well do it to you?

Daywork Near a Bend in the Tennessee River

After Charles Wright

Mouths to feed, dear Lord, mouths to feed.
We cannot eat those bald cypress knees,
Pockmarking and puzzling the shallows, nor
Drink from this current, swift with summer rains.

It shoots the poison arrows of water moccasins,
Carries our detritus to the sea, washes clean
The murky creek beds of our conscience.
All that's left is just shamefaced labor

In bright rows of cotton, soybeans and rice.
The swatting and sweating for filthy lucre.
And here, cresting the cliff, a bald eagle
Dive-bombs the white-capping surface.

He pulls in a rivercat, child-sized, struggling.
Snatch me up in your tree-tall talons, Lord!
Lift me high above the browbeating sun.
Pick clean my weary bones in some glory land!

Bedtime Story Redux

Listen up, my dear ones. These days
Grow fangs and bark and drool.
They reek of woodsmoke, wet fur.

The past is a rancher's coil spring trap
We all get snared in. Let the howling
Begin! Someone should call the cops

To say it wasn't me. Someone should
Phone the landlord to complain
About the weather. Somewhere

Keeps stretching rubber-band-like
Beyond our driveway. If I could,
I would cosmic dust you far away

To the other side of dreams. There,
We would truth each other. There,
We would feast upon hearts of stars.

Bar Napkin Love Letter

I never know when to stop. Moon
Goes down, sun comes up. North wind
South wind. Alarm clock chimes five.
Ice melting on a blade of grass.
You beside me should mean forever.

You're beside yourself without flowers.
In my dream I'm beside you snoring
In that cold and shabby bedroom
Where we fall asleep clutching books.

If my time left is a high desert to cross
Barefoot like some heartbroken Apache
Your laughter will be a raven's caw.
Your name will be two river pebbles
Held on my tongue to ward off thirst.

Despite or Because of the Bourbon

This flivver parked inside my chest
Refuses to crank. I fold and unfold
And eat the road map with hot sauce.
Daddy speaks of souse meat. He worries

Up the weather. *This here exit is the exit*
You say as we pass by the exit. Daddy
Speaks of cancer, oak leaves in gutters.
My third eye sparkles like a Kmart

Christmas star. Daddy speaks of car wrecks,
Radiation seeds, sparrows. Black Jesus
Break dances while White Jesus weeps.
I pray myself to sleep and dream hellfire.

Day After Christmas Blues Poem

And this shall be a sign unto you—
You shall find the leftovers wrapped
In aluminum foil, lying in the refrigerator.
Another gray morning sky, another
Hangover of biblical proportions. Dirty

Dishes, the unlit tree. Two crows rummaging
Through gold and green wrapping paper
The wind blew against the back fence.
Three sheep beyond the back fence,
Standing still in their field, standing

In the manner they've always stood,
In the manner they always will,
Their gentle breath fogging upwards
Only to dissipate. A blessed sun
Beyond gray sky, rising only to fall again.

The Only Apocalypse

Time is neither young nor old,
but simply new, always counting...
—Wendell Berry

There is a dove on its morning wire
Announcing this very moment,

And I want it to mean something,
Something heavy, as the longhairs used to say.

I want it scrawled in some virgin's blood
All over the cave walls of my mind.

I want it etched into the skulls of our foes.
I want it read in the tea leaves, preserved

Inside every tree ring. I want it bannered on high
From that skywriter's prop plane. I want it

Polluting the groundwater, black as cake
From the old Kentucky coal. I want it

Shouted all at once by the business-suited
Millions on their sidewalks and subways,

In their limos and taxis and Learjets, shouted
As some one-syllable mantra, the quick

Cough from a punch to the solar plexus,
The question to all of our answers.

from
RED CLAY JOURNAL

FutureCycle Press, 2018

A Small Town Epiphany of Sorts

Sweet little slash-and-burn moments
Teenagers flush with wonder a night

Sky ignored from the mall parking lot
Those full moon evenings cruising

Riverside in a three-hundred-dollar
Datsun oldest among us driving slow

Way too slow windows down cigarette
Smoke a raging wildfire of cuss words

Of squeals tape deck busted FM college
Radio experimental jazz music shooting

Stars music of cellular growth/death
Of blood of meat music of backseat

Thighs touching sweaty hands music
Of honeysuckle-scented nighttime air

Misting upon sweetgums upon pines
Those highway lines faded streetlamps

Burnt out headlights killed this Asian
Contraption swerving left then right

To this very day I am still swerving

Blues with a Feeling

Somewhere in the back
Of my mind,
A deep-rutted dirt road muddied by
Summer thunderstorms. High weeds
Greenstriping
The center. On one side cotton making, on
The other, soybeans.
A sparrowhawk *keer-keers*
Overhead. That train
Crying from down the tracks, back
Near town. My mind shrinks
A bit each day; each night I pray to
Nothing. It shrinks a bit more.
A puddle in the hot sun,
Soon a wet spot, a drop of blood on
The thorn-pricked finger.
A pinpoint, a chigger. Where the chigger was.
Through the eye of a needle
That road passes, muddied from
My mind's thunderstorms.
I swear I hear that sparrow hawk,
The train. I swear that road will
Deliver me.
I'm not there yet, no not yet.

Lines Composed Upon Hearing You've Touched Down Safely

Who are these that fly like a cloud,
and like doves to their windows?
—Isaiah 60:8

O my peregrine beloved, you storm cloud chaser,
You blue-sky gypsy! I can finally exhale to whisper
A prayer of thanks to any and all deities above,
Below, make-believe or not. So what's a few
Temporary longitude ticks between lovers?
If you promise to stop looking for my doppelganger
In every shitty small-town bar, I'll do my best
Not to end up sans pants in the backyard again,
Soused, whistling for those screech owls.
On a brighter note, I've collected a handful
Of your hair, and this poem is dedicated to it.
And those cats swear they see you chasing fireflies
In our driveway. And that pillow still preserves
Your skull's curve. I'll curl up beside it tonight
To count jets instead of sheep. Sleep instead of weep.

Watching Myself in a Movie Never Made

Drunk. Beestung in the backyard.
Finding myself beneath blackening billows,
Wildfire smoke signals waiting
To be read. Losing myself
Like a leading man
Scanning sky for some impending doom.
That smoke, a sort-of premonition,
A what's to come for us all,
And those stingers, those barbs left behind,
Little reminders to tread lightly,
To keep yourself to yourself,
To absorb the poisons and absolve
Those who administer them.
A low humming from the hive,
Its lesson in the swelling.
And this set looks real enough:
Old live oak, loquat tree, birdfeeder,
A neighbor's dog barking. Get my chest
Puffed out, my chin jutted
Towards the daylight-waning danger.
But I fear the world sees me
As just another bumbling gaffer—
T-shirt, jeans, ass crack showing.
The leading lady appears
With ice pack, with pills, with that
Method actor's mask of motherly worry.
So I take to the deep shade
With venom in my veins, with woodsmoke
In my lungs and hair. There will be no
Run-throughs, no take two. There will be no
Awards ceremonies, no speeches.
And when credits roll
Up Yonder, who will lock up
This abandoned theater? Such tiny bees,
Such smoke, such a poison in my heart.
Sky lowers, lowers
Again, turning itself to ashes.

Writing the Same Poem Over and Over Again and Expecting Different Results Each Time

For Albert Einstein and Thomas Piper

Those days long ago, sun-bright and summer-sweet.
Cicadas droning us both
Down a cattle path.
I want to say cotton high, but most likely
Soybean, canola or wheat.
I want to say
A red-shouldered hawk keening,
A buzzard circling, the neighbor's harelipped boy
Pulling a knife, cussing us. I want to say
A crop duster crashing other side of the highway.
This cow pasture earthquaking
For a moment. Flames
Five stories high. Smoke, sirens.
I want to say we find a body in the creekbed—
Dry the creek, bloated the body. Limbs
Twisted, face bluish-white. Maybe a schoolgirl I liked.
But instead
We stroll home for suppertime
Clutching coins train-flattened. I've been told
This is trite, this is too southern. I've been told
To dig down deeper,
Get my pampered hands dirty in memory's muck,
In the death-smelling humus
Of the past. But goddamnit, that crop
Duster landed safely, that harelipped boy is home
Studying on the New Testament.
That schoolgirl's body was never found. We could smell
Field peas and cornbread.
The pennies twice their size in my pants pocket,
A treasure from some
Other time,
A currency we could never spend.

Let Them Have Dominion

"...over every creeping thing that creepeth
upon the earth."
—Genesis 1:26

Early August midday heat fields
Of corn rattling ears dry-roasted

Inside husks ears of a young boy
Nearby dirty from play in a sand-

Swept backyard the boy's daddy
Down in mines the daddy's daddy

Corn-drunk on the porch mother
Scrubbing underthings polishing

Brogans wringing an old rooster's
Neck he pecked the boy one time

Too many strutting the dirty boy is
Dragging this little carcass tied by

Twine to his left foot dragging across
The swept sandy yard zigzagging

By the pens old rooster gone limp
Eyes blank talons tracing lines

Over the yard a roadmap a map
Of tiny roads all crisscrossing

Tiny roads all leading nowhere

Discovering a Noble Truth in the Backyard

Charred end of August, oven-dry heat
        lifting out of Mexico. Too much sunlight, for too long.
A dove coos once in the live oak, then again,
                the last time till spring. Your drink-cooled hand

Finds mine, and I hadn't realized mine was lost.
        Something gets caught in the throat, inaudible,
Ineffable. Something, someone might say, better left unsaid.

                To understand that everything must go, sooner
Or later—you and I, the dove, the oak,
        the whole goddamn shebang—it's not the later
                        that bothers me, but the sooner.

Worried Man Blues

The afternoon sky had turned
All West Coast or something,
And summer was seeming to say
"Sorry for everything"
By way of breezes and gray clouds,
With a few teardrop pigeons
Falling from the Biology building,
Coming to rest or to roost
In some hedges I'd never noticed.
So I burrowed down deeper
Into the debtor's prison
Of my day job, and I thought
Of all the songs I wish I'd written.
And I played a few of them
Inside my head at low volume,
So as not to disturb those voices
In their slumber. But several
Woke anyway, and one sang
A ballad to silence the rest.
It was heartland in its origin,
Full of working-class sadness.
I've counted ten thousand verses
With no sign of it stopping.

Born Again Homecoming

Therefore, their sons grow suicidally beautiful
at the beginning of October, and gallop terribly
against each other's bodies.
—James Wright

High up in the bleachers on some
Friday night in America. Each
And every one of us high
On this euphoria, this distillation
Of the moment. Each and every
One of us high on pharmaceuticals
Of some sort—our collective
Gray matter conjuring starbright
Lights, the crowd's death-chanting,
The padded warriors in military
Precision, the glittering queen
And her small-town courtesans.
Yesterday, today, tomorrow
Forgotten. It's as if we all decided
To exist, daydreaming each other
In our sad drab team colors, all
Cheering on cue, the young men
Pounding each other's flesh
Down into the field, this earth
Most certainly not spinning.

The World Is a Vast Place, Full of Wonder and Irrelevance

A mosquito-bitten afternoon, thunder
Again to the south.
An overcast overgrown
Afternoon, a snakebit afternoon.
Sitting here,
Sucking the venom
Out of another workday.
Sitting here, counting my blessings and curses.
Found objects—
Live oak, one raindrop flattened
On the grill cover,
A dead leaf, other dead leaves,
Tumbler of bourbon, hawk on the wire.
Red-shouldered, I think.
Staring me down, daring me
To trespass
On his airspace, to clash
Beaks and talons. May the best
Predator win. I sit back,
Smiling at his screech,
Scratch an elbow itch and think—
What's the ratio of humans to raptors?
Another screech and I think—
What's the ratio
Of spirit guides to venture capitalists?
The hawk takes off, all noiseless
And ghostly.
Sitting here, sucking bourbon
Out of the tumbler,
Spirit-guiding the thunder, the rain.
Staring myself down, daring
Myself to trespass,
And to forgive those who trespass against me.

Over the River and Through the Woods

Dogwood trees slipping into
Their little yellow
Indian summer dresses. Sun-bright
Hillside thickets shine
And blur just off Highway 43.
Up Spruce Pine Mountain,
Then Hawk Pride.
Windows down, radio low,
Bangs lifting
In the breeze. What exactly
Would the Indian summer breeze say
Concerning the nature of
Passing on by, passing on through the thick mist
Of years. What was it
Grandmother said about wanting to go home
To be with her Lord? Everlasting.
Seems it's all the same old tra-la-la,
The same fiddle whine
And buck dance,
The same sad miner's refrain.
She turned one hundred that September.
Her breathing machine, her house
Full of kin.
Each and every assisted breath a prayer
Of thanksgiving, a prayer
For mercy. Glory Hallelujah,
The killing frost, the strong Amen.

The Known Unknowns

I thought he might slip me the answer.
—John Lennon, explaining his helicopter ride with the Maharishi

At the exact same moment astronomers
Discover another universe, not parallel
But damn near the same as ours, my
Large thin-crust four cheese extra
Garlic with side salads becomes
One minute late—two times.
Free delivery, it says right here
And also, way over there. We inhabit,
Of course, this slightly crooked
Carbon-based copy. All of our
Ice Capades, beauty pageants, boy
Bands and suicide bombers, atrocity
Facsimiles light years away from
The originals. Seems it lets us all
Off the hook. My hand wringing,
Your shower singing of show tunes.
Our lost elections, championship
Games, virginities. And I cannot
Stand it when they don't slice all
The way through the pie, then forget
Those little parmesan packets. Also,
How hard news keeps happening,
How weather keeps changing, how
Time talks hush-toned sense to me
Like some hangdog sober friend
At the New Year's Eve party.
Or to misquote Robert Pinsky—
When I have nothing, it will
Not be a moment too soon.

Mapping the Daydreamt River Valley

For Paige Andrew

Begin with the high-flying bird's perspective,
With the hard winter sky's perspective.
Shade in the sad sloped edges—

Tupelo to Tullahoma, Belle Mina
To Botush. Show sunlight glinting off
Cattle ponds, off the lakes and tin roofs.

Show flooded fields of soybeans.
Show pineywood hills
And mill towns. In your legend,

Denote tributaries, sloughs, water levels,
Indian mounds, moonshine stills,
Pet burial sites, Klan headquarters,

Snake-handling churches and pool halls,
Those little roadside crosses
And all the underage drinking spots.

The river dammed up with tears.
The river dreaming of man-sized catfish.
The river, the valley, the vulture above.

Projection unknown, coordinates useless,
And the scale is a secret
Someone forgot to tell you.

Four Blood Moons, Nothing Has Changed

The wife and I in our old hometown,
Night of the last blood-
Supermoon.
Early autumn Alabama night—
Rose-scented, somnambulant.
The driveway concrete cool to bare feet.
My parents laughing in the front yard
Like children, like old lovers.
This darkness, it seems,
Hides one's faults,
Not only outside, but in.
The moon in our binoculars
Is a communion wafer
Dipped in a tempranillo,
Maybe the same vintage we received
At dinner.
Sangre de Christo! There's no man in the moon.
If this tranquil evening scene
Is some metaphor
For something, it's beyond me,
Beyond my field of vision, beyond
Our lone satellite.
The immensity of it all, the immensity,
Makes some people believers
And others skeptics.
My wife goes in to retrieve her camera,
Leaving me alone
With the *mater* and *pater familias.*
A child once again,
Gazing out to where forever ends.
Everything orbiting, gently orbiting.

The Father and the Son and Canadian Geese

Everything blurred by mist and fog—
The bog, the man and boy, the park
Trail behind them, this flock honking
Their arrival south, the towering
Oaks, elms, sweetgums, leaf-stripped,
Tiptops lost in low clouds. The boy's

Grip tightens on the man's hand.
With the other he lifts binoculars,
All but useless. "A shame not
To see them," says the man, "after
Such a long drive and all." But the boy
Squints, leans a tobogganed head

Forward, swears he can see shapes
Shifting in the distance, ghostly gray
Images flashing in and out of fog.
The boy keeps quiet, mulling over
That this must be his imagination.
"A shame not to see them," the man

Repeats, "after such a long drive."
The honking sporadic, then stopping
Altogether. Hum of a nearby highway,
Drip-droppings upon dead leaves.
A woodpecker drumming. The boy
Inhales, holds his breath like a secret.

Mapmaking: The Middle Years

The day begins cloud-shrouded, then clears.
My mind, however,
Holds onto its mist, its doom and gloom.
I skim through each and every
Odd moment looking
For some footnote, some reference to the work
As a whole. Only leaves, gusting leaves,
And those unnumbered pages
Of beloved souls
Lifting up to The Beyond.
Daddy rides his brakes, fidgets
AM radio, sings out—
Detour, there's a muddy road ahead.
He sings out—*I'm heading for*
The last roundup. I unfold
Our roadmap to find us off the grid.
No coordinates,
No projection, no contours.
And legend has it
All these named places have no place names.
Transcribe the birdsong,
Windwhisper.
Lat/Long the first thought best thought.
In his ninth decade
Daddy is almost invisible,
And I'm not too far behind.
The day ends clear, then cloud-shrouded.
There's a muddy road ahead.

The Buddha Way Is Under Everyone's Heel

A friend tells me she was born in Year of the Dog
But her mother would've preferred the Pig.
Little yellow elm leaves tickertape
Our slow parade to lunch. Traffic slithers by
On its belly. "Year of the Pig," she said.
"Good fortune and wealth and so on."

This is somehow troubling to me, as we stand
Like terra-cotta warriors waiting
For the crosswalk signal. Why long to be
A different person dwelling
In another time and space? We're all basically
Sad-assed, doomed. And as her mother would say,

"Existence is suffering." And as my mother
Would say, "We wished that you lived closer."
Now that I think of it, hell, I do too.
I wish that I lived closer. Closer to intentions,
Closer to daydreams, closer to that
Rawboned prisoner rattling this skin cage

I've locked him inside of. I want to say
All of this to my friend, but the light has changed
And we step ahead with all the other travelers
And my birth was in the Year of the Monkey
And most mornings I wake as a hungry ghost
Longing to pass on to the next realm.

A Requiem of Sorts

On the verge of something great and terrible,
We are. You and I, the whole hominid horde.
Maybe this ends in fire, in water, in space debris.
And don't get me started on noise pollution,
Which is why I keep going back to the classics—
Nighthawk chirps, the odd rainfall patter,
Gulf breezes rustling Chinese tallow leaves.
And lizard-brain me this, my sweet sister
From another mister, if deep inside each of us
Is contained a whole other world, unique
And unexplored, what's the use of fretting
Over this one? This blue blip in the bang
That was big. This eightball spinning towards
Some cosmic corner pocket. This watchmaker
God's dimestore candy with its hot lava center.
Guess I'm not making myself clear. If only
I had perfect pitch and a dead composer's
Powdered wig. If only I could sing exactly
What I want to say. If only these wings
I've sprouted would unfold and flap
And fugue me up to that Far Far Away.

Aubade for Yet Another Day

The morning is, whether I want it to be or not.
Slips through the open window with birdsong.
Hangs before me like some painting forgery,
Like a cracked bathroom mirror displaying
My backwards message forwards. Morning
Redrums me with its squeaky child voice,
Sports a seventies haircut, blood-red sweater.
Morning clambers out of a cold muddy creek
And splashes us all with its wet dog fur.
Morning watches its weight, never hits snooze,
Checks weather and traffic before stepping out.
Morning unfolds itself like a Triple A roadmap
Awaiting the cinnamon-sugary muffin crumbs,
The inevitable coffee rings. And try as I might,
I cannot find that cutoff road to the afternoon.
Try as I might, I cannot fold morning and fit it
Back inside the rental's glove compartment.
Next exit—fifty miles. Jesus on the radio.

Hawk Pride Mountain Nocturne

The deceased leave behind their voices.
Some in shoeboxes
Stacked in the back closet of the mind.
Others under creaking steps,
In birdchatter, water murmur, highway hum.
Most, middle of the night, seek us out
With their quick-and-dead singsong.
Disembodied, tremulous,
Gusting down
Off the pine-sided hill.
An uncle's high tenor; an aunt's thick alto.
A whole ragtag church choir from beyond the beyond.
Voices pure as light,
Light as breath. We breathe in these voices
In our sleep,
Taste these voices in the bittersweet
Draught of dreams. Voices
In the shapes of clouds, voices raining
Down the old mud-trodden hymns.
Horse-and-buggy us
Back to that little white church
In the woods.
Lay roses on those headstones carved with our names.
Sing out, brethren, in voices
Long silenced but still heard, harried
By a north wind from the past.
Let your praises pillow our slumber
And greet us like morning mist.
Hearken us back from our dreams, brethren,
And forward into the light.

Summerpoems

First of July

A single cirrus cloud hanging
Outside the breakroom window
And I'm ten again, tasting
Honeysuckle blossoms,
Hiding in a copse of trees
Ringing the old north pasture.
Cattle at the pond, katydids
Chirring up in pine boughs,
Low hum of tractor-trailers
Out on Old Memphis Road.
Two vultures slice the cirrus
As a nearby phone rings—
Those greens and those browns,
Even those blues fade
And I have no answer
For whatever question is coming.

Second of July

Yesterday's cloud a no-show,
So I radiate leftovers in a little
White box. Sugar ants single-file
Along the sink's edge, seeking
A drop of water, a sense
Of purpose. That midday sky
Is glaucous, threatening
With infinity, and a cedar elm
Catches my attention,
Waving like some old friend
In a crowded auditorium.
I wave back and it keeps
Waving, so I wave again
And it's still waving.
So happy to have a friend.
So lucky to have no soul.

Third of July

Only so many ways to say
"I love you"—just one
In fact—and I whisper it

Nightly into the bathroom
Mirror after my daydreams
Have all been strangled
In the bathtub like Grover
Norquist's starved government.
And high above my head,
High above my rooftop,
Those Mexican free-tailed bats
Consume their own weight
In gnats, flies, mosquitoes,
While high above them all,
Beyond satellites, light pollution,
A star burns out in response.

Fourth of July

At the neighborhood cantina,
Tequila-shooting. Thunder-
Storm, rain off to the east.
Eyes closed—seeing sparklers,
Roman candles, smoke
Bombs in my childhood street.
Smelling grilled meat, hearing
Mother's cackling laughter.
Another shot—sweet nectar
Of the gods, the gods of brown
People, nectar from God's lightning
Bolt striking spiky desert plants.
No gods in our neighborhood
Though, no rain. Just head-
Lights flickering on the off ramp,
Wisps of smoke, unheard prayers.

How to Talk to Kids About Death

Appear at midnight, out of nowhere
Like some snippet from a dream,
But leave your wig and clown nose
Back at the office. Chuckle softly,

Toot your silly little horn. Start
With interpretive dance, then
Throw in Tuvan throat singing. Sit
Cross-legged at the foot of the bed,

Beatnik-snapping your fingers.
Warm their tiny, sticky hands
In your big fat bear paws, gently
Squeezing to accentuate words

Like *love* and *loss* and *defibrillator.*
Finish with a flourish of French
Surrealist couplets, and by no means
Answer any questions that arise.

Emergencies in My Meditation

A gray sky lowering to smother us all
On my little lunchtime break.
That Frank O'Hara hour—
The long sidewalk stroll,
A hamburger and a malted.
I'm composing a poem for you, Frank,
All up inside my brainpan.
A rambling free-verse epic
In Esperanto, mostly,
Concerning those cracks
In the sidewalk, that gray sky
Low and smothering,
The absence of birdsong, squirrel chatter.
O the sad things we jot down!
O this minor key sonata
Of an afternoon!
Pianissimo, my friend,
Pianissimo.
Frank, just look at how this world
Has turned out.
Inside-out? Not even close.
More like outside-in. All shadowy,
Black hole-ish. Everything
Reeking of burned-out stars.

Clouds and Moon are One,
Valleys and Mountains are Distinct

Picking clean the bones of yet another afternoon.
Fighting for scraps of memory's feast,
Whatever crumbs fall my way.
Another Monday
Working for the state, climbing
Those high hills
Of forms, reports. Recalling something
Wang Wei wrote—*Alone in the empty forest,*
I have an appointment with clouds.
Recalling Daddy, myself,
Decades past
Atop Mt. LeConte, springtime,
High country springtime.
My teenage scowl, I'm ashamed to say,
Offset my father's
Countenance, his beaming countenance.
It offset blooming rhododendrons,
Soft wash of sunrise
Bleeding up from the Carolinas.
What I would give to be there again,
Treading through the cool wet alpine grass,
As close to a heaven as I'll ever be.
What I would give to reach a switchback
And hear Daddy sing
"The Great Speckled Bird," hear him whistle
"Steel Guitar Rag." But on the
Other side of the breakroom window,
An overcast sky has been duplicating itself
For weeks now. Also,
Same redbud tree, same corner chair, same
Fountain pen and pad.
I can no longer see those springtime mountains,
Even when I close my eyes.
And these bones, these same old bones,
Just about picked clean.

Drinking Moonshine with Father-in-Law

At some point a mason jar appears on the cutting board
Filled with clear liquid squeezed by some good old boy

And as it sparkles like that corner Christmas tree he says
This is one part Colbert Mountain branchwater trickled

Through cool mossy limestone bluffs one part Alabama
Red dirt corn mash two or three parts Dalton family

Blood sweat and God knows what so I have to ask
Which part burns like hell and makes me want to fight

But after awhile the bright lights dim and I cool off
And don't mind all those rudolphs santas and elves

Snowmen and marys josephs and christchildren
So we drink a toast to holiday cheer and we sup

And we cheer and we sup and can't see clear to put
The lid back on or open gifts or go to church so I nap

It off and dream of wild turkeys strutting calling in a hilly
Back pasture where someday they'll sprinkle my ashes

Running Late to the Centenarian's Funeral

A mild morning. Fog shrouding the farmhouses,
Fields of winter wheat.
A few oak leaves left. Hawk on a fence.
This highway is new to me,
Skirting north
Of Bankhead Forest.
Brother-in-law driving without a license.
Sister and children fidgeting.
I'm in back counting silos, counting
Hawks upon the fence.
I'm in back sleeping with eyes open.
I'm here and not here
On a highway new to me, not new to me.
Confederate flags, gun-show billboards.
Filthy truckstop bathrooms. *Ribbed for her pleasure.*
All roads the same road,
Someone must've said. Same farmhouses,
Same fog, same hawk on a fence.
One hundred years past,
One hundred years from now, what does it matter
To that pine-bristled hill,
To that low leaden sky on the horizon?
We are all hurtling down
The same highway fast asleep,
Each of us to wake soon enough.

Mhoontown Cemetery, Colbert County, Alabama

Last day of the year. Sky gone bloodless, color
Of bone, texture of tombstones.
Daddy and I off the Natchez Trace,
Pulled over to read the names.
John Mhoon. Henry Pride.
God called thee home. He thought best.
What little daylight
Waning with the Indian hen's cry.
No other sounds, no
Highway hum, no train rumble.
Just the Indian hen's cry.
Then Daddy clearing his throat, saying
"*Mary Mhoon*
Born seventeen-fifty-eight
Can you believe that?"
Spitting snow now, right above freezing.
Flakes the size of summer gnats.
I don't believe much of anything these days,
Which seems to be a problem.
Plina Borden. Mose Spivey.
Gone to a bright home where grief
Cannot come.
Dead center of this plot, atop a hillock,
An old water oak's twisted remains
Pokes its palsied fingers
Into the blind eye of The Maker.
Since thou can no longer stay
To cheer me with love,
I hope to meet thee again
In yonder bright world above.
No peace out here, no eternal rest.
No lessons to mull over.
But there's food and wine back at the house
And another blank year in the queue.
Out on the highway, heater blasting,
Laughing at Daddy's gallows humor.
T. S. Hall. Clara Gilbert.
I have crossed the river. Meet me in heaven.

Nobody Knows You When You're Down and Out

There was a child down the well and the chicken coop on fire.
That blizzard in March and a crack in the slop jar.

There was Daddy on the bluff right before he slipped off.
Bear Creek dried up and the small pox and the croup.

There was Billy Ray, Lovely Lloyd, Big Bill and Bum-Bum.
There were verses from the Bible and Kool-Aid and crackers.

That flood on my birthday and a knife in my arm.
There was the coming of electricity and the going of angels.

There was Mother in the choir and a song I would not suffer.
Ticks to burn off on our ankles and calves.

There were pencils and papers; there was dust on the swing set.
There were blackberry brambles by the old tower ruins.

There were guns under the bed, forgotten and unloaded.
Sheet music of Handel, and I fell off the monkey bars.

That song on the radio with the long slow fade—
"Hey Jude," number one the day that I was born.

There was a river and a lake and a pond and a creek,
A boat and a cooler and blood bait and poles.

There was this world all around and the one I created.
I'm going there soon; I will never come back.

from
MY HEAVENS

FutureCycle Press, 2020
Winner of the FutureCycle Poetry Book Prize

My Heavens

With the deepening darkness came rain
Rain with its despondent whisperings
Rain threading itself

Through the lowering sky, through
Leaves slumbering / Rain
Stitching itself into dreams

And dreadful imagery / Dreams
Disappearing as soon as they were dreamt
That sound of my breath a prayer

That clock on the wall wearing my face
At long last, it stopped
At long last, the rain slackened

Then stopped / The sky
Raised up on its haunches and howled
The whole world shuddered

And slunk back into its hole
Somewhere a pamphlet proclaimed
This was the first day of the rest of my life

One Man's Purgatory

And so it came to pass that nothing much happened.
Light and darkness and climate fluctuations.
Species evolving and a dance craze here and there.
The rains eventually falling, but mostly elsewhere

And of little consequence. I sang myself awake.
I could feel eternity like a pebble in my shoe.
I curled up inside that cabin of my soul

And awaited word from a world gone deaf and mute.
Sometimes a songbird in the dream out the window.
Sometimes a sunset that my mother would've loved.

All in all, it worked out fine. The ballet of leaves.
That bedtime story of shadows. My good ear
Cupped to the cold pane of midnight, almost catching
Some whispered secret from over the horizon.

Alabama Field Holler

I have decided to blame no one for my life.
—Robert Bly

Winter morning all hollowed out,
Whistling its one-note ballad.

Morning bark-stripped, sanded-down,
Held over a flame. A woodsmoke

Morning piping clear across
Back pastures of my childhood.

Let me wake early to cop the riffs
Of this bygone morning song.

Let me stomp out with snare drum
Past Granddaddy's electric fence.

I'll get in tune with morning, root
Myself down into the hard red clay.

I'll call a blues to myself in 4/4 time,
Stand back and await the response.

Render Unto Caesar

That big game long past, long lost.
The stadium filled with wind.

A multitude of lights left burning,
So bright they can be seen

By all the gods, myself included.
My songs unwritten. My hair

Grown long in dreams, in legends.
Let us slip through the parted curtains

Of this moment, fellow traveler.
Let us leave it all behind for others

To reconcile. Off-and-on rain showers
And the possibility of chance.

Sleepwalking. Metallurgy. Memory
Is a dollar-store jigsaw puzzle.

Unsteady Lines

Thunder me back from the murky edge of memory.
The schoolyard at false dawn,
The uncut grass flash-frozen. Dog-bitten
And damned beside the drought-dry creek.
A mouth filled with music.
A fever high from blood reckoning.

I believe dreams grow on the north side of trees.
I believe in someone else's time,
In someone else's weather.
I believe in a deity unbelievable,
Raking us all over the coals
To prove some pointless point.

What a strange smoke scent this morning,
And I keep trying your number.
Just the sound of lapping water, of perch
Popping in shallows.
Throw out the lifeline, throw out the lifeline—
Someone is slipping away.

Vignette for Frank O'Hara

The Indian summer afternoon was bleeding out
On its flat-earth stretcher
With no hope of resuscitation,
With no priest for last rites.
And something about that play of light

Slanting through yellowing leaves
Made me want to ouija board my grandmother
For folksy instructions on canning,
On preserving the last of the season's okra,
Field peas, squash and peppers.

But my workmate was before me,
Swirling her worries around inside a coffee cup,
So I found myself listening to
But not really hearing whatever it was she sang.
It sounded like verse/chorus/algorithm.

It changed keys into a bee's drone.
It slow-faded to some commercial break
For new cars and trucks with no money down.
Then the weather report and its magical realism—
More of the same, more of the same.

Broken Arrow

Such an utter mystery, this day-after-day.
Dog alarms, cars barking,
Oak pollen upon the blank page.

Jet planes arcing from nowhere to anywhere.
Sweet surreptitious sighs
From wet root and vine. Clouds

Like monks on the mountain path of sky.
Why, oh why these gnats
In my backyard whiskey? The afternoon

Floating facedown in a golden ennui.
Every day a holy day to anticipate,
To religiously observe.

The transubstantiation, the utter mystery.
I swallow it all
And expect nothing in return.

I believe in the zero sum of Before + After.
I believe in daylight on the windowsill.
I believe another drink is in order.

I salute whatever part of my soul that still wanders:
Pontotoc, Winnemucca, Thrall,
Broken Arrow. That little piece of my soul

Fixing a flat outside of Fort Worth.
The south wind whispering its one promise
In the greening prairie grass.

Missing Inclement Weather On a Sunny Afternoon

The sky intoxicatingly blue. Sky gone
Payday drunk, tipsy
With its own sense of the infinite,

With its own
Weightless heft. And just last week
Those low clouds conspired

To keep us all hunkered down,
Shoe-gazing,
Scurrying like ants from shelter to shelter.

I hid in my room for days, jotting notes
In Esperanto, shuffling about
With tissue-box-slippered feet.

All the while,
That biblical rain spoke in tongues I could
Almost understand.

Sounded like idle threats in old ballad form.
Sounded like Earth's epitaph
Recited in Babylonian. The telephone

Became my silent partner,
The grocery list an epic poem.
I had never felt so alive.

Incidental Music

A low hum in the background of everything.
Low hum and the click track of hours.
I pan myself to the left, then right.
I pull the faders on a long workday.

Satie and his snuff box. His long fingernails.
Bo Diddley and that loaded pistol
On the passenger seat.
All hits. No filler.

The world plays out in mono.
The world demands its guarantee up front.
Both sides of my brain backstage, muted.
There will be no encore.

Blue Norther

Such muted music of overnight weather.
The heart's metronome slowing,
Largo, largo. Such lackluster litanies,
Such a cacophony of thought.

A harvest moon gone jaundiced.
Trees talking in their sleep.
I am at one with nothing,
Neither nothingness nor somethingness.

I am scratching and clawing
At the storm windows of myself. I am
Staring down the hall
Into Mother's room. Her journals,

Her jewelry, her hair on the pillow.
A light that we see
We think we see. It soon enough fades,
And we forget.

All the Way Home

Our future selves in a field of sky.
A field of light, a field of electrons.
Here we are. There we were.
Whatever was dreamt absorbed.

Whatever was left of darkness absorbed.
Everything expanding
At a rate of something to something.
Nothing lasts forever and only nothing.

The dance is set to begin. The dance
Of no remembrance.
The dance of light and electrons.
Of this, I am almost certain.

Colbert Mountain Sutra

We wake all of a sudden beside the dream's fire.
Smoke-shrouded, moon-haunted.
Dream of the dreamless,

Dream of bones and hair. The fire
Of what's-to-come.
The fire of whatever-will-be.

The fire moon-haunted and all of a sudden.
We hem and haw; we till our bloodless soil.
We thumb rides

Along some celestial highway.
Riven, our words, our shallow deeds.
Riven and tattered

At the charred end of a hard day.
O for a thousand tongues to sing,
They sang and they sung,

And it stung our memories
Like bees after first frost, like static
From the pump, like love

Before the loss of love.
This old world, the weight of a stone,
And all that we know

And think that we know,
As inconsequential as an eyelash
On my sleeping mother's pillow.

Epiphany in D Minor: The Saddest of All Keys

It was all a bit different this time around.
The cafe, the coffee, those hominids
Sitting next to me. And the sizes,
The shapes of various rain puddles.
The wind most certainly not whispering.

Staccato grackle-squawk in fast 9/8.
Those schoolchildren outside the museum
Oddly quiet, their wizened little faces
Scrunched up in past-life pain.
Friends and family, truth be told,

Still friends and family, but altered
Remarkably at the molecular level.
Like online photos tinted sepia
For sappy effect. I, of course, was
Rock-of-Gibraltaring my way

Through all of this. Haunting
That old corner table, scrawling
Future police sketches of everyone,
Eavesdropping for the good
Of our nation. And then it hit me.

Apropos of Nothing

Feeling like death warmed over,
I discuss Dickinson with a coworker
And swear I hear a fly buzz.
Some kind of racket going on here.
Some play of light
Early in the day, early in the year.
Sky smeared white, sky postmodern
And over itself.
I'm playing possum in the supply closet.
I'm searching for something
Beyond the breakroom window.
I'm rubbing two coins together
And reciting the state pledge backwards.
And just over the horizon,
Halfway to heaven,
Daddy nods off in his recliner.
His hands two mourning doves
At roost. His face a mask
Bathed in the orange glow
Of televised atrocities. His dreams
Becoming more and more real.

What are the Odds?

Still wagering with this ghost inside me
That our shadowy old world
Cannot last much longer.

Another morning steaming deep
Inside the cracked cup.
Another dream left at the curb.

This ghost inside clawing to get out,
Chicken-scratching for forever.
This ghost adored

For his manifestations, his expressions,
His primitive art scrawled
Upon the cave walls of my ego.

And this tired husk finds itself at times
Beyond clouds, sipping soda
Beneath the blue edge of heaven.

Hedging bets from a turbulence prayer.
A skeleton seen within the stewardess.
All engines fail eventually.

Tishomingo Sutra

Cicada drone blue-sky dharma afternoon.
Everything beginning to fade around the edges.
Everything going the way of the old family farm.
All shadowed stories and hearsay.
Hushed chatter from the back pews.
I still climb those pines of childhood
For a far-off glimpse of future,
For that suggestive caress of oblivion's breeze.
My speech has become sticky with sap,
Untranslatable and in love with itself,
My heart some folded road map
Misshelved in the hometown library.
Eyes on the prize. Hands across America.
There is no pond without its reflection.
There is no going without the return.

High Harmony

Evening filling up the sky like a river rising
In the lock of a dam.
My heart risen to my throat. My heart
A barge heavy with necessities,
With frivolities and the like.

Those old folks long gone.
Their shape notes long gone.
Whole years pass by like parades
No one heard about.

I could sit out on my back steps
To empty a bottle and count the miles
Between lightning and thunder.
I could insist that the world
Follow me down a dead-end road.

Instead, I stay inside
With Grandmother's quilts
And her rusted knives,
Not believing a word the radio says.

Never Enough to Go Around

High holy processional of thin cirrostratus,
Of cumulonimbus and chemtrails.

Sunlight turns itself down a notch.
Wind dies alone atop some faraway hill.

Even birds ground themselves,
Hushed in supplication.

I take to the city streets like a stray dog
On any Sunday.

Last year's gutter leaves. Memory's detritus.
This fellow on my bus

Holding his own against the gods,
Against time and space,

Against the nature of being.
I blink once and the world has changed.

I change my mind
And the world stays the same.

Stranger In a Strange Land

Tossed in sleep like a man lost at sea.
Awakened
To another unmapped island of a day.
Odd squawks of babbling blackbirds.
A subtropical
Sun toasting my tender skin.

Some strange whispering patois of wind
In tall grass, in leaves,
Leaving me speechless, disoriented,
Unsure of what to do next.
Just keep spinning in space, no doubt.

Just keep plotting coordinates,
Jotting down field notes.
Just keep bringing bright beads and baubles
To that fearsome native tribe.
Their dialect indecipherable; their
Customs beautiful and frightening.

Without Knowing Why, He Followed

After Barry Hannah

Somebody hollering in the Delmar Baptist Church.
Hollering meat and muscle. Hollering heaven.

Somewhere, the Lord is walking
With a limp and a cane.

He's down the wrong side of the road
Waking up coon dogs.

He's in the middle of a cemetery at midnight.
Confederate stillborns. Oak stumps.

Poison sumac around the edges of everything.
His bottle gone empty, the morning

A lifetime away. His night sky
Just sheet music no one can sight-read.

Umbilical

A storm forming on the other side of the river.
Some storm like a simile
But the river literal.

Winds whitecapping the water,
And I am a child.

I am a child as the sky turns biblical.
I am a child born of rain and cosmic dust.

Long before Old Testament God,
There was wind and water
And the other side of the river.

There was the child I am
And the child I am becoming.

There was the beginning and the end.
There was no excuse for what came next.

Pass/Fail

Sometimes there is a shadow within shadows.
The end of a dark hallway
And nothing more.

This haunting of head voices,
These remnants of dreams
Like scraps of cloth across the face.

We see the past in field glasses
Hovering high like some bird of prey.
We hear grass grow, soil settle.

We shiver from the chill of someone else's tomb,
Our names and places
Wiped from that schoolhouse map.

Thunder in the distance,
The playground empty.
This will all be on the test.

Caught by the Indian Summer Train

I keep missing the exit for that hometown in my mind.
The borough in broken pieces
Scattered on the other side of the tracks.

They're waiting up for me, I know,
Fretting, hand-wringing,
Frittering about the fried pie table.

That porch light with its congregation of moths.
That harvest moon like a Buddha
Atop yonder ridge.

The leftovers. The folded quilts.
Those sepia ghosts in their dollar-store frames.
Evening deepening,

Sinking down to get comfortable.
A lone dogwood hunkering up against the house.
It leaves little flames flickering,

Its afterglow some sort of metaphor
For the fire we return to,
For the ashes sprinkled upon our slumbers.

Suburban Ephemera

I have a degree from the university of oblivion and I'm as empty-handed as the shirt on the clothesline.
—Tomas Tranströmer

Wonders upon wonders other side of this windowpane.
I cannot explain nor deny them.

Clouds begin their mysterious journeys.
An anole gray on the photinia's trunk.

Butterflies like solar flares drip-dropping among tropical flowers.
Flowers gaudily colored as if by a sightless child savant.

The palm tree swaying, writhing.
Puffed air cooing through the dove's throat pouch.

I crack the window to hear mown grass chant its single-note mantra.
I sit back as thunder rattles the spoon in its coffee cup.

This chair holds my frame.
This frame holds my heart.

This heart has a door that's been slowly opening for years.
Down the hall I can see that there's nothing yet to see.

Gnostic Poem for Maurice

I am almost ready to catch fire and pray.
Almost done with mystery,
Almost fatigued by this flat-tire fate.

I am almost river, almost red clay,
Almost that song sung
By the side of Mother's grave.

And what a beautiful hoax: forever.
What a slight-of-hand,
This late-winter afternoon. The air

Like a lover's breath, blush
Of redbud blossoms, green parakeets
Squawking on the power line.

Everything simpatico with the sense
Of its senselessness. Everything
Inhabiting its own preposterous heaven.

Homesick Ballad in C Minor

Tuned and plucked by the plectrum of time.
Opening riff of west wind
Rattling the high tupelo branches.

Bobwhite. Whippoorwill. Low hills
Wreathed in woodsmoke.
Slow music of rain upon the singing river.

A theme develops from the formless form:
Fencepost hawks, barbed wire down,
Patterns in the quilt on a dead woman's bed.

Thunder takes a solo. Last verse, last chorus.
One time I lay in a summer pasture
And watched the sky become itself.

Pretty Mouth

Hung upside down in an old sweetgum.
Hogtied. Bend of the river
Autumn. Almost frost.

Bled out by those workweek wounds,
By those little day-in/day-out barbs.
Tried to ask for a last cigarette

But could only snort
And whinny, could only chomp
These molars. What's left of my spirit

Gutted, tossed to those blueticks
Yowling by the fire.
Hogtied, bled out and gutted, eyes

Open to the lidless sky. I thought death
Would just be darkness, but it's
More akin to the color of woodsmoke.

Fifteen Minutes in Heaven

On your state employee-mandated break time,
Visit the charming courtyard
To sit in and doze off on bright winter afternoons.
Sunlight warming the benches and chairs,
Filling up the space
Between buildings. Buildings rearing up
Into endless blue.
Passing cumulus puffed up
Like baby-fat cherubs, like obese angels.
And don't bother with a book
Or coffee,
Just bring the Self to lose through nonthinking.
O potted perennials!
O sugar ants filing forth!
Leafless trees starting to stir and sap,
Each falling drop sparkling like an ice pellet.
From the nearby clock tower
An hour chimes.
A peregrine falcon shrieks.
That's your shadow there on the pavement
Begging you to stay forever.

Ornithology 101

A rude north wind spring morning. A blackberry
Winter morning. A baby bird of a morning.

Today sits peeping on the edge of its nest.
Today has its beak wide open, waiting

For whatever the world might shove down it.
As a child, I kept a fledgling

Brown thrasher in a Keds shoebox
In the washroom. Daddy dug up worms

And grubs to pamper it for days,
And I soon came to resent all that attention,

All that nurturing he gave the little bastard.
I know that time makes orphans of the lot of us,

But that cold wind today is the reason
I'm telling you this. Also, my teeth ache.

My back aches. And these shoulders ache
Where my wings should be.

Incidental Water Music

Why not return to those sweet streams of adolescence?
There is no one here to stop us. No one at all.
The garden hose, the swimming pool,

That cattle pond dragonfly-dotted. Granddaddy's
Chaparral creek
Swollen and somber with late winter rains.

I find myself often at a bend in the dream's river.
I find myself lost
Along the banks of these blank pages.

There is something to water besides life
And its elements. Something
Beyond death, and it reflects among the reeds.

I am thirsty for the past but I keep drinking future,
The present
Flowing fast inside a riptide of others.

There is something to water and the memory
Of water. I keep coming up for air
But forgetting to breathe.

Old Time Religion

I want a poem I can grow old in. I want a poem I can die in.
—Eavan Boland

Can't seem to recall that last conversation
But take comfort in the fact
That our mother/son voices beamed out

Into the heavens,
Then back down into each other's ears.
Voices of the heavens. Heavenly voices.

I pick up the receiver now and again
For time and for temperature,
For telekinesis and wrong numbers.

I cup my ear to the morning mirror
And catch myself in a familiar lie.
I drift off on occasion

To the church music of meadowlarks.
They are piping in that old pasture
Where the coon dogs are buried.

There was, and is, and will be eternity.
I believe in it now
Because I've heard it singing.

from
A RAIN ANCESTRAL

San Antonio Review Press, 2022

Silent Witness

As nightfall came, all the shadows
Stitched themselves together
Into one immense funereal shroud.

Birds became skeletons
Displayed upon bare branches.
Daydreams spun in their little graves.

The TV and the radio
Stopped working,
For which I was grateful. And

One street over,
Either a car backfired
Or someone was shot to death.

I said nothing to no one,
Figuring that sooner or later
My time would come.

Meta Love Story

On the way to the grave I met a woman.
A real catch, they all said.
Legs of a showgirl, hands of a rancher.
Heart like a stone
At the bottom of the sea.
She built us a home
Out on the cold hard prairie.
She tucked me in at night like the child
We never had.
I wrote her ballads—evenings, weekends—
And disappeared slowly
As was my nature.
She brightened like a star to engulf
The both of us.
We're happier now.
We burn in darkness.

No Hands Clapping

Almost dark of a false dawn light.
Dry gust of west wind.
Sundried redbud leaves spin
And clatter down
Like a peasant child's toys.

Last night's whiskey still mixing it up
At the cellular level.
No breakthrough in my meditation.
No lesson learned
Living to see another sunrise.

I'm ramping down on cause/effect.
I'm gearing up
For all that future nothingness.
Spin and clatter, grasshopper,
Spin and clatter on the short way down.

Blood Brothers Revisited

A coworker says *blackberries* and I'm ten again
In that bramble beside the pasture.
Tom is barefoot and giggling.
Our lips purple from the ripe fruit.
I carry daddy's binoculars
And his sense of impending doom
Around my sunburned neck.
Mosquito hum. Meadowlark mantra.
Far-off rumble of the Memphis train.
Our sticky fingers. Our aching bellies.
That sky a blueline map of forever.
Tom pulls a pocketknife to swear an oath
For all gods listening or not.
He slices our palms and we touch
For the transfusion. We touch
To mingle meanings. We touch, then let go.
Decades have passed, that pasture
Now a neighborhood,
Yet I can still taste the tartness
Of a childhood Saturday. I can still hear
Those meadowlarks, the mosquito hum.
I can still see the scar,
And feel that faintest pulse
Of a dear friend's summer heartbeat.

Rest Measure

A ringing in the ears on the Ides of March.
A quivering of the spirit,
A glissando of sorts.
Some humming of that tuning fork
In the center of the soul.

And through an open window wafts
The major-thirds of a dove's coo,
Then silence. Such the silence.
The silence of grandmother's voice,
Of mother's voice.

The silence of sleet melting
On a sun-warmed street.
The engine killed. The wind dying down.
Far-off thunder
Awakened from its daydream.

That last chord struck
On the old parlor piano, years ago,
Still dissolving
Into the dust-shrouded air.
D minor. The saddest of all keys.

The Old Country

There on the map but vague in my mind.
Blurred through the window
As we touch down in rain.

Rain like some shroud to be lifted.
A rain ancestral
And singing of pity.

This is the dream that will happen.
This is how it will all play out.
There will be seagulls

And pints of stout and my face
Around every corner.
There will be you in the air

And you on the ground.
There will be us in our cups
At the end of the bar. Sad ballads

To drink in the lingering light.
Welcome home, perfect strangers.
Welcome the heaven of peace.

To Andy at the Crown Liquor Saloon, Belfast

Ornate these windows stained—a sinner's cathedral
For quiet, lasting peace. Across the street
That oft-bombed station sits, but here you pull
Our first abroad refreshments. Pints of stout
And whiskeys neat. Correct response, you say
To ice or water. Not lagged by jet just yet,
We cheers and quaff. We marvel at the way
Our lives have brought us here, amazed, in debt
To you, kind sir. I'd like to pass away
Inside this bar old Betjeman preserved!
The Protestant hooch, the Catholic stout, my belly
Not troubled, just ceasing fire and full. I'm led
To love this place: no television, no music.
Your hands upon the taps a magician's trick.

To Tim in No Man's Land, Belfast

Surprised to hear your brogue requesting bourbon,
We turn with eyebrows raised. I cannot take
That boggy water of life, you laugh. My kin
Will never know. But friends beside you poke
And take the piss to diss all night. You're smacked
That Yanks would ride a bus up here. No strife
For now, you sigh, but picture sidewalks flecked
With blood, with brains, and snipers on the roof.
We sip our silence, reverent travelers. Your home
Is gapped between those troubled Ulster tribes.
You slur Kentucky in your throat. So time,
It heals, but schools still segregate. And bombs
Are made in other places, but children grow
To hate the Other. We pay our tab, then go.

McHugh's in Belfast, Founded 1711

We pour ourselves into a back booth
As the trad music begins.
My ragged breath
Inflates the bagpiper's ego.
My glass had whiskey. Now it doesn't.

The afternoon passes like a gypsy's cart
As that fiddler reels
Some peat bog melody. Something
From the mists and the rocks
And the heather,

Something from the Scots soaked
In stag's blood and milk.
I will die for this song.
In a field beside the sea I will die
For this very song.

My bones hollowed-out and whistling
In the wind. A dirge for the days
I can no longer remember.
No spirits, just smoke.
Just smoke in the heaven of sky.

Mother's Day, County Down, Northern Ireland

We empty our pockets of quid at Quinn's
And take our full bladders down to the promenade.
Magpies and jackdaws laughing.
Kelp the color of my younger man's beard.
A small rain gathering atop the high peaks

And Slieve Donard flexes above us
Like a crofter's hard bicep. Mourne Mountains
Sweeping down to such a sweet surf, as you
Point out sheep and seagulls along Main Street.
I mourn this holiday as is my old country custom—

Grieve and drink. Grieve and drink.
I weep and gnash my National Health teeth.
Let us turn our backs on the village of Yesterday.
Let us sing along with Mother Water.
Hear her murmuring in each crashing wave?

To Pat Behind His Desk at the Donard Hotel

And here's that mizzly weather you predicted
Just yesterday. The Mournes are crowned with clouds
Of Nordic nature. *Mizzly,* you grinned then said—
A mist and drizzle mixed. Those Irish moods
That we had hoped for: gray and low. McGinn's,
You roar, will pour the proper pint next door.
The best in town, turns out. We bird the Glenn
And thereabouts for thrushes, gulls, and more,
But thirst sets in, and soon. Those stouts go down
Like mother's milk and just as nourishing.
Upon return, we fill you in. That clown
We'd left behind comes up—bada-bing
This orange nightmare presidential mishap.
You misquote Chomsky, then tip your woolen cap.

To That Odd Fellow Bellowing in the Dundrum Bus Station

Someday I'll sip your share of grief, my friend
And fellow traveler. Your tattered sweater and smoke-
From-burning-peat discolored hair. You bend
Those clichéd Paddy rules—a jacket Nike-
Emblazoned, charity shop-acquired, I'm sure.
The wife and I gaze down to let you pray
Your moans in privacy. Others stare:
Amused, disgusted. Begging's not your way
It seems, just whiskey weeping. Stout atonement.
I'm just about to cry for drink myself,
But here's our bus to Newry. You sit and slant
Across the aisle for several miles as if
The world has tilted, then pull the cord to stop
In nowhere's middle. *Sláinte,* sod and sheep!

Leaving County Down

From the Newcastle bus we spy Savage's Pub
In the Castlewellan square,
Exactly where that fellow in McKen's
Said it would be.
He had pulled our pints the night before
And peered into your past.
His granny a Savage from thereabouts.
His voice a drunken piper's drone.
He rubbed stubble
On what could've been your father's face
And spoke of many more about.
Savages. Ulster crofters
With France in their veins.
Our stouts settled.
The air in the room settled.
Liverpool vs. Somebody
On a muted corner telly. Your mother a Stout
And your father a Savage, and now
I'm holding your hand
On this day bus to Dublin. So many names.
So many names stacked
Like gray stones in the fallow fields.
And those green hills rising up,
Daring us to believe in them.

To P.J. Murphy at Sweny's Chemist

A shop the size of Joyce's piney box
That's cool and quiet to boot. Your darting eyes
The gray of gulls. Moher. Your longish locks
A necromancer's white. I've crossed the seas
To seize that fabled lemon soap, to tune
A folk guitar and hear you strum, caress
That ballad from *The Dead.* Of Dublin town,
Encyclopedic knowledge you possess:
The previous names of pubs and such. I grab
A book or two, then strain to follow suit
Our conversation. This southern gift of gab—
Your Cork, my Alabama—plays on and out
Until I ask about your namesake stout.
Try Mary's Bar, you grin, off Grafton Street.

Hallway Divertimento in F Major

Hotel Mont Clare, Dublin, Ireland

On my hung-over way to the corner chemist
For your NSAIDs and ointments,
For my antacid tablets and Band-Aids,
I find myself paused—in awe—
Outside our next-door neighbors' room.
Their afternoon duet has drawn me in
With its rudimentary rhythms,
With its haunting, high-pitched
Biological imperative. Upon each uhh and aah
I blink like some smalltown Baptist
Beholding midnight French cinema.
No DO NOT DISTURB sign dangling,
No housekeeping staff in sight,
So I take one step closer
And imagine my musical role within a trio.
O those little youthful deaths to mourn!
O bittersweet autumn of the bones!
The back goes. The sap slows. And you
In our room having a headache lie-down.
Tempo quickening, pitches rising,
But before the performance can climax
I shuffle off towards the elevator.
And later, after dinner, the two of us
Will sit up in bed holding hands,
Falling asleep to some old movie:
The car chase, the fireworks,
The bullet train penetrating its tunnel.

To Larry Ducey Driving in His Weather

Our final Irish morning lowered temps
And somberly rained. Those days and days of sun
Had dazzled pasty locals. They'd shed their tops
And basked like gila monsters spread upon
The desert floor. But now, our luggage stuffed
And in your taxi's trunk—Old Dirty Dublin,
Goodbye, we say! Adieu to Sweny's: closed.
Adios to Davy Byrne's: closed. The M-1
Is sparse this early, and heading north, you speak
Of recent snows and mizzle. You've come to love
That low and graying gloom. Your inner clock
Is winding down, you say, so stop and lave
It all of doom and rest beside your fire
With tea and smokes. O blessed, sodden Eire.

State Worker's Skeptical Bedtime Prayer

O Lord, methinks I'll call you Lord. Are you
Affixed up there on high, or somewhere else?
And us lowdown in murk mistaking blue
Above as heaven, hell beneath cool grass.

It matters not to me, as I assume
Some gods cannot exist except in dreams,
In trifling songs. I guess most folks presume
To hear from you by way of simple hymns

Or over-the-counter meds hallucinations.
My mood's been altered by rum. I'd like to mellow
And spy just once, you, big fellow. Creations
Upon creations! So, might I feast on crow?

This bottle's full of nothing. I'll say good night
And find the faith to know you'll get the lights.

State Worker Swears Off Local News

My morning ramble crosses a creek, the place
They found that murdered girl. O Lord, we need
Some answers right away. Behind each face—
Just ruthless animal urge? A dark, indeed,

An evil core to all? I'm tired, so tired
Of talking to myself instead of you,
Which turns out is the same. How weird
Yet natural our synapses flaring blue

In prayer, in dreams, in blinding rage or love.
But where were you, almighty? If everywhere
As some do say, confess to this and save
Us all our grief. Let's strip your altar bare

Of monster-fingered idols. In fits and starts
We'll keep such things to ponder in our hearts.

State Worker Considers the Concept of Dualism, Then Shrugs It Off as Metaphysical Smoke and Mirrors

Again with lightning bugs and blooms. The grass
A resurrected green that dusk deepens,
Enhances even. Blinking, blinking no less
Realistic as mushroom trips, sci-fi zines.

The bedroom window cracked, my lover's breath
Upon my throat, and Coltrane keening, shrieking
From down the hall. It's either this or death?
A heaven. Hell. Am I to lay here begging

Forgiveness of sins? And just what sins are those
But ones of survival? Nature; nurture. Science
Is on my side for sure, but cannot close
The deal, blast one past the outfield fence.

So thanks, I guess, for nothing. Maybe thanks
For separating thoughts from what one thinks.

State Worker Catches Himself in a Lie, Then Realizes Truth Is Far More Interesting

It seems I've always been the praying sort,
If prayer is weeping along with FM songs
Upon the lonely road. That human heart
Will break in slow 4/4; the rights, the wrongs

Of childish lyrics; mélange of minor chords.
And all those setting suns I've spoken to
Intoning grace. Amen. Muttered words
That disappeared like smoke into the blue.

And birds, blossoms, breaking waves don't know
They're holy, perfect relics of a heaven
Existing only here, only now.
Just thank that winter moon, that summer sun.

Just thank those family photos on the shelf.
Just thank the stuff of stars you call yourself.

State Worker Ponders His Life, Which Turns Out Is Just a Facsimile and Not Legally Binding

This weather's odd for early May. A sky
As gray, autumnal-like as Hallow's Eve
With chilling wind for budded leaves. Don't try
To cipher meanings, plot and graph the jive

Of boundary demarcations. All talk is small
It seems, inconsequential, belittled
Before this vast creation. Sometimes I feel
Like Christ upon his cross: expired, naked,

And right about most everything. Methinks
I'll clamber off this Calvary for bagels
And breakroom coffee, and later, liquor drinks
To toast our pitchfork-wielding angels.

Who cares that time does not exist? Let's down
These whiskey replicas, then paint the town.

State Worker Files Himself Away to Forget That Any of This Ever Happened

Such peace. Such boundless peace down here between
Out-dated forms, reports. That soothing hum
Of after-hours vacuum cleaners. I'm in
Like Flynn, gone triplicate with sheets-of-time,

Evaluations, memorandums. Then—quiet.
An afterlife of sorts. No messages,
No calls from friend or foe or kin, albeit
Was never one to stay in touch. Who rages

Against these dying lights? I shut them off
A long-ish time ago. Such boundless peace
In hanging folders hung. I used to scoff
At documents, the ticker-taping vice

Of clerks, etcetera. But maybe heaven
Exists in cabinet-form. I'm paper-thin!

Leaf Raking Afternoon Koan

I find myself ankle-deep in red oak leaves.
Little drops of blood.
Little drops of bye-bye now.
Mother's sky is overarching in Glory,
Always expanding,
Blue and vast in its blurred beyondness.
Mine is shrinking, shrouding
Head and shoulders
Like the shawl of some smoking peasant.
I sweater-fold my sky
At the dusky dark end of a workday
To place on the shelf
With all other sundries. I drift off
Into wine-sleep.
I snore my prayers and awaken godless.
Mother sings to her sky.
The very memory of her voice
Shakes the grass blades above her.
Who am I to question memory or voice?
Sky or oak leaves?
Caught between tomorrow and yesterday
I am, wrapped
In a shawl of sky, smoking,
Shuffling through the blood-red drops,
Becoming a memory of myself.

Palm Sunday Phone Call

That tired Lenten voice of my faraway father
On the other end of the line,
Weather-beaten and weak,
Faint but full of forgiveness. His voice

Is an almost holy relic
In its ninth decade. His voice
Riding into the village on an ass
Under the scrutinous centurion eyes

Of the past. A crowd gathers round,
Disembodied and bodied. I hear them
Beeping in on the other line.
They are colleagues and family,

They are students and loved ones.
They reach out to touch the hem of his garment.
They weep and they gnash their teeth.
And I am by the side

Of his long and meandering pathway,
Waving those green fronds
Of pride and of envy. I, who have led
The peasant's life of a hapless onlooker.

I, who will leave nothing behind
But a thin shroud of what-ifs.
The stone not rolled away.
Nothing much to be saved.

Made for TV

I stand tall in the prairie grass,
Final scene of a movie never made.
Smoke signals. Wildfires

On the horizon.
A dove coos one last time.
Lonesome dove.

Last of the Mohicans.
I squat in a clearing, chewing
Mescal beans

To envision all those gods
I created. I hum
The closing credit's theme.

I lie down
In the shadow my life cast.
I would like to thank the academy.

Lepisma Saccharina

Mother would flip through the leafy folds
Of her old family Bible as silverfish
Swam up the spines with tiny legs
A Creator surely did not give them.

She would point her stubby finger
At the still living and the long dead.
She would click her tongue with bug sounds
And say—Would you just look at that.

She'd say—Lord he was a handsome thing.
She'd say—Mean as a snake that one.
She'd say—Hey boy, gimme some sugar.
But it was salt she poured

In an older man's wounds. Any man's.
Neighbor. Pastor. Son-in-law.
Her husband gladly worked three jobs
Just to stay out of the house.

His skin grew as thick and hard
As exoskeleton. He lived on dewdrops
And the dried glue of days. In time,
He grew wings but never learned to fly.

Buried Alive on the Old Chisholm Trail

Something went wrong beside the dry creek.
A late winter sky reborn in its own image.
The neighbor's radio buzz, the four-lane drone,
Etcetera. Amen. I have my soul pressed up

Against the cracked living room window,
Seeking out that shaggy buffalo vibe.
I've made friends here in the temporal world.
I've heard ghosts down inside the stereo.

The past is not your friend, someone sang,
The future not your enemy. And my hair
And my fingernails of late have grown longer.
There's a tang of prairie upon my tongue.

The After Afterlife

By the time you read this I will be gone.
Gone in the sense of not here,
Gone like a train
In the song of the same name.
Long gone, forgotten gone, the getting
Good and gone.

This is not a note left for loved ones.
This is not a cry for help,
Nor a shout into the abyss.
It's just that
Sundays can smother you with a pillow,

Roll up your corpse
Inside a Persian rug to drop
Into the metaphorical river. Gone
I said and I meant it.
Gone my cellular structure.
Reordered and replicated and processed

By someone else's hazel eyes.
Overheard down the hallway. Overlooked
In the morning mirror.
My shadow cast on that sidewalk bending
To the hard luck heaven of nowhere.

NEW POEMS

Risk

Hung-over Ash Wednesday. Back patio.
Again with the redbud blossoms,
The doves cooing.
That Russian oligarch blue jay
Squawks and whines
About sanctions on the tray feeder.
Fuck him and the crows.
The world is going to hell.
The world should go to hell.
The world is hell already.
Such a strange city, these clouds.
Patchy blue sky. Exotic. Otherness.
I plan to visit this city someday.
A busybody tourist
With an out-of-date map,
Asking for directions to heaven.

The Known Unknowns (Slight Return)

Once in college I cheated on a psychology exam.
I might admit this (under oath)
To a shrink
If she would flash me her long slinky legs
And stop waterboarding me.
I'd say—My workaday face has become
A Chinese puzzle
And all I have are the French instructions.
She would pull up her skirt and giggle.
Make it rhyme, *sil vous plait?*
There's no time, anyway.
The inner workings of my mind—
Or anyone's for that matter—
Do not interest me in the slightest.
Puzzles, riddles, prayers and ballads.
Even cheating, I barely passed that class.
All that time and tuition spent
To learn that my ass is still grass.

Tossed Off Adagio in G

Hell-hot midsummer afternoon.
A horse latitudes afternoon, a past
Is never past afternoon.

High cirrus clouds hung up
Motionless
In a sky stagnant blue, sacrosanct.

Everything heat-shimmering.
Everything a faded facsimile, coded,
Indecipherable, obfuscated.

Our memories, our thoughts,
Heat-shimmering
Skyscraper-reflected facsimiles.

All is passing beyond the eye's
Doomed detection.
It's for the best, this is.

Such a tiny tragedy, each moment.
Time's telling triumph.
There is now, and there is not-now.

All of us hung up high on now,
Floating in why. Dig
The coded cloud. The stagnant sky.

Once More with Feeling

I am that child always beside the poem's creek.
Barely a trickle in August.
The same poem, the same creek.
Always cicada buzz. Highway hum. Noon sky
The white-hot threat of Old Testament god.
Daddy kicks up an arrowhead,
Then another. Chickasaw. He speaks the word
Like a blessing, like a curse.
Granddaddy stoops down to snatch up
The poem's water moccasin. He cracks it
Like a whip, the tiny head flying off
Into drought-dried bramble.
And all the women back home, too busy to bother
With the same poem, the same creek.
Too bone-tired to assuage
The same sad-eyed old boys. Too proud,
Too practical to acknowledge past, or future,
Or even all the days of all the years
Curving out before each of us.
A deep-rutted gravel road not on any map,
Twisting, turning, going nowhere.

Precious Memories, How They Linger

A bird is singing somewhat tritely
Atop the dream's billboard by the highway.
The dream is real, and the billboard
Reads—*Hit A Pole?*
A cartoon car crushed and smoking.
A cartoon sky with a bird singing tritely.
I recognize the ad's number
But cannot get cellphone service.
I recognize the birdsong
But cannot place the exact species.
According to mnemonics, the bird goes
Say something...Say something...
Having never hit a Pole
(Or a Slav, or an Irishman),
I find myself forgetting bird songs
On a daily basis.
But the dream is real. My father is real.
He scans the hometown daily
For dead people he might know.
He keeps outdated food in the fridge
To stay connected to the past.
The past is never past,
It's not even ketchup anymore.
My sister comes to visit.
The three of us dream the present
In which we display old family photos
And a 1-800 number
On that billboard by the highway.
Real cars and real trucks
Blur past, filled with future ghosts
In the present tense.
They keep ringing up our number
But we let the machine get it.
Say something, it says. *Say something...*

Accidental Man

Everything I have ever learned
(Such the tiny sliver of knowledge)
Will flash and fade soon enough.
Everything I did not, as well.
Firefly thoughts. Lightning bug

Memories. Starlit dreams
Dimming on a dead man's bog.
Look how our hatred
Grows like exoskeleton. Our guns
Hanging limp with ennui.

Better for us all to step backwards
Into the sea, grow gills and fins.
Better to retreat to those cold depths,
Leaving only the victory of wind,
The victory of birdsong.

No Soliciting

Both of us standing alone beside each other.
The sun in our eyes.
The moon in our hearts.
Both of us wishing to die first,

Me with my drinking, my reckless driving,
You with your fatty steaks,
Your family history. But just beyond,
The abyss yawns. Ho-hum.

How boring nothingness must be.
Possibly as much as somethingness.
And those sepia childhood forever fields
Fade fast regardless,

While both of us live incognito,
Dancing the dance we cannot dance.
Our hearts in our eyes. Moon in the sun.
The abyss beyond, still yawning.

Participation Trophy

For Dean Young

Such horrible advice I have received
And shall receive yet again.
Be all that you can be. Dance

Like no one's watching. Just do it.
Midnight in the cemetery, and
I'm painfully sober being all I can be.

You are all winners!
I shout to those cold wet headstones.
No one is watching

So I foxtrot past the graveyard,
Whistling. I just did it.
I came to inside this simulation.

It was whatever I set my mind to—
Work's drone, vacation's hassle,
The doctor's waiting room. Magazines.

People. Time. Life. I did
What I had to do but mostly did not.
Nothing special about existing,

Even less about not-existing.
I don't know exactly how to end this,
But then it's not really up to me.

Acknowledgments

These poems were published in the following journals or anthologies, to whose editors grateful acknowledgment is given.

Arcadia Magazine: “Despite or Because of the Bourbon”
Atlanta Review: “The Glass Ceiling”
Barely South Review: “Backmasking Presentation, United Methodist Church Youth Group”
Big River Poetry Review: “Villanelle for Bloodbait”
Bone Parade: “A True North Dream with Astronomy and Botanical Consequences,” “Bar Napkin Love Letter”
Boxcar Poetry Review: “The Father and the Son and Canadian Geese”
Broad River Review: “Born Again Homecoming”
The Broadkill Review: “Emergencies in My Meditation,” “Running Late to the Centenarian’s Funeral”
The Cape Rock: “Stranger in a Strange Land”
Chattahoochee Review: “Mapmaking: The Early Years,” “A Requiem of Sorts”
Cold Mountain Review: “Call to Prayer,” “The World Is a Vast Place, Full of Wonder and Irrelevance”
Concho River Review: “A Correspondence of Sorts,” “Lepisma Saccharina”
Cumberland River Review: “Still Life with Gibson SG and Unpacked Bags”
The Dead Mule School of Southern Literature: “Tent Revival on Hawk Pride Mountain,” “Billy Sherrill Borrows Granddaddy’s Martin Acoustic”
December: “Day After Christmas Blues Poem,” “Let Them Have Dominion”
Extract(s): “Lines Composed Upon Hearing You’ve Touched Down Safely”
Foliate Oak Literary Magazine: “Crazed Man Changes Weather”
Fredericksburg Literary and Arts Review: “Broken Arrow,” “Caught by the Indian Summer Train,” “Incidental Music”
Free State Review: “Colbert Mountain Sutra”
Gnarled Oak: “Worried Man Blues”
Good Works Review: “One Man’s Purgatory,” “Unsteady Lines,” “Homesick Ballad in C Minor”
In Stereo Press: “Waiting for the Fire to Go Out”
Jabberwock Review: “Ornithology 101”
Josephine Quarterly: “Are You Washed in the Blood?”
Juxtaprose: “Nobody Knows You When You’re Down and Out”
Kentucky Review: “Discovering a Noble Truth in the Backyard”
Kestrel: A Journal of Literature and Art: “Epiphany in D Minor: The Saddest of All Keys,” “Suburban Ephemera,” “State Worker Files Himself Away to Forget That Any of This Ever Happened”
Kindred Magazine: “Summerpoems”
Midwest Quarterly: “Watching Myself in a Movie Never Made,” “Leaf Raking Afternoon Koan”
Mississippi Review: “Blues Dreams”
Monarch Review: “Last Blue Yodel”

Nashville Review: "Pantoum from Wilson Pickett Interview"
Natural Bridge: "My First Rally," "A Medium-Sized Theology"
Oklahoma Review: "Early Recordings Vol. 1"
Oxford American: "Confessions of a Southern Dandy"
Painted Bride Quarterly: "Alabama Field Holler," "Hawk Pride Mountain Nocturne"
Potomac Review: "Writing the Same Poem Over and Over Again and Expecting Different Results Each Time"
San Antonio Review: "Blood Brothers Revisited," "The Old Country," "State Worker's Skeptical Bedtime Prayer," "State Worker Considers the Concept of Dualism, Then Shrugs It Off as Metaphysical Smoke and Mirrors," "State Worker Catches Himself in a Lie, Then Realizes Truth Is Far More Interesting," "Buried Alive on the Old Chisholm Trail"
Southern Humanities Review: "Do This in Remembrance of Me"
Tower Journal: "Aubade for Yet Another Day"
Tulane Review: "Crazed Man Changes Weather"
Typishly: "Vignette for Frank O'Hara"
Weave Magazine: "Born Homecoming Friday"

"Never Enough to Go Around" first appeared in *Anthology: Chicon Street Poets* (Lit City Publishing, 2017).

"The Known Unknowns," and "How to Talk to Kids About Death" first appeared in *The Great American Wise Ass Poetry Anthology* (Lamar University Press, 2016).

About FutureCycle Press

FutureCycle Press is dedicated to publishing lasting English-language poetry in both print-on-demand and Kindle formats. Founded in 2007 by long-time independent editor/publishers and partners Diane Kistner and Robert S. King, the press was incorporated as a nonprofit in 2012. A number of our editors are distinguished poets and writers in their own right, and we have been actively involved in the small press movement going back to the early seventies.

Each year, we have awarded the FutureCycle Poetry Book Prize and honorarium for the best original full-length volume of poetry by a single author that we published that year; if no original collections are published, no prize is offered. Introduced in 2013, proceeds from our Good Works projects are donated to charity. Our Selected Poems series highlights contemporary poets with a substantial body of work to their credit; with this series we strive to resurrect work that has had limited distribution and is now out of print.

We are dedicated to giving all of the authors we publish the care their work deserves, offering a catalog of the most diverse and distinguished work possible, and paying forward any earnings to fund more great books. All of our books are kept "alive" and available unless and until an author requests a title be taken out of print.

We've learned a few things about independent publishing over the years. We've also evolved a unique and resilient publishing model that allows us to focus mainly on vetting and preserving for posterity poetry collections of exceptional quality without becoming overwhelmed with bookkeeping and mailing, fundraising activities, or taxing editorial and production "bubbles." To find out more, come see us at futurecycle.org.

www.ingramcontent.com/pod-product-compliance
Lightning Source LLC
LaVergne TN
LVHW020046110826
845155LV00029B/652

* 9 7 8 1 9 5 2 5 9 3 4 3 7 *